A FRAMEWORK FOR LEADING

The Top Level

DWAINE CANOVA

The Top Level

Establishing a highly functional and structured top level is essential to effectively grow and operate a business. Many early-stage and emerging-growth organizations delay or fail to properly implement a top level. The leadership gets wrapped up in daily happenings and doesn't establish a proper leading infrastructure, making it hard to grow.

This book is a conversation between the principal leader of an early-stage company and a leadership coach. The leader is eager to accelerate the growth of the relatively new company. The leader explains some of the issues in the company and the desire to strengthen the leadership and management team. The coach explains the need for a framework for leading and managing that will put the needed structure for growth in place. The principal leader is curious but skeptical and needs to be convinced that the proposed solution will work in the company.

Becoming aware of the missing or incomplete top level needed to grow and become a larger company provides unique insights for readers. Readers are encouraged to engage with the thinking that leads to a decision to start using the methodology. Join in the conversation and connect with those issues that are important in your organization.

Also by Dwaine Canova
Overcoming the Four Deceptions:
In Career Relationships

The Series:
A Framework for Leading™
Improve leading and managing in your organization.

Books:
A Framework for Leading:
Simple—Easy—Effective
Building a Foundation

A Framework for Leading:
Advantages
A Managing Methodology for Leaders

A Framework for Leading:
Connect and Align
Communicating in High-Performance Organizations

A Framework for Leading:
Expectations and Outcomes
Dream, Explore, Anticipate

More books are coming in this series.

We believe...

Having passion for the *why* of the organization is essential.

Deliberately implementing a top level for the organization provides an overarching covering to hold the framework together.

The organization's structure for how it is to operate must begin at the top.

Structure reduces stress and conflict.

Structure makes it easier to innovate.

Structure increases performance and productivity.

Shared use of integrated online tools brings people together.

A FRAMEWORK FOR LEADING™

A Series of Books

Improve leadership and management in your organization.

by

DWAINE CANOVA

Objective: Improve the leadership and management capabilities, capacities, and outcomes in small and midsize businesses (SMBs).

Symptoms: Few organizations really thrive. Many struggle and are characterized by poor communication, chaos, and anemic growth. Of the one hundred million American workers **30** percent are engaged and inspired, **20** percent are actively disengaged, and **50** percent are not engaged.[1] Also, **55** percent of small and midsize businesses fail before the end of their fifth year and **70** percent by year ten.[2] Of venture-capital-funded companies, **75** percent don't make a return for their investors.[3]

Problems: Leading and managing organizations is difficult. Building the new capabilities needed for growth isn't easy while coping with the demands of daily operations. Too much time with daily hot issues traps management into ongoing firefighting mode. The result is no time available to establish a leadership and management structure. Leadership by seat of the pants happening on the fly is cause for alarm.

Solution: Implement a structured and holistic approach to lead and manage your organization. Getting organized first with what you already know and do makes leading easier, efficient, and more effective. Implement this simple and easy-to-use leadership and management structure. This is the foundation for profitable and sustainable growth.

Results: Expectations include accelerated growth, higher margins, fewer failures, and more successes through increased productivity and performance. Work environments become more collaborative and less stressful.

Audience: People in organizations dedicated to improving their leadership and management capabilities and outcomes.

The books in the series do not need to be read in a specific order. It is hoped readers will be drawn to a particular subtitle and topics that suit their interests and then set their own reading sequence to match with their needs. However, the first three volumes are intended to introduce the basic concepts with discussions about applying the framework and methodology.

It is hoped the reading will be done as the concepts are being applied. In this way the learning evolves in a manner and pace that suits the reader. There is overlap and repetition with some themes between books when needed to reinforce and expand certain concepts.

This is our form of "Street" learning and teaching. It emphasizes your daily experiences as the primary source for learning. The framework guides you with practical online tools, structure, and concepts to identify and solve issues and implement opportunities as they occur.

[1] Gallup Research
[2] United States Small Business Administration
[3] Shikhar Ghosh, a senior lecturer at Harvard Business School

A reason for being...

Inspire Vibrant Life and Excellence

Why?—How?—What?

Life should be exciting and fun in organizations. Each individual is super important. Vibrant life is created by establishing an organized leadership and management framework. This makes for a healthy environment in which people work together better. An easy-to-use methodology and related online tools make it happen.

> **Why?**—Inspire vibrant life and excellence
>
> **How?**—Establish organized leadership and management that mitigates chaos and conflict
>
> **What?**—Methodologies and online tools

This series of books and its related materials combine as a prescription to improve leadership and management in small and midsize organizations. It helps for-profit as well as nonprofit entities. It begins with establishing structure and processes at the top level and continues with it for all levels. This makes it easier for individuals to...

work together in harmony!

A Framework for Leading:
The Top Level
Motivate with Purpose—Execute with Structure

Final Printing by CreateSpace.com
Printed in the United States of America
ISBN-10: 1512045276
ISBN-13: 9781512045277
LCCN: 2015907219
CreateSpace Independent Publishing Platform
North Charleston, South Carolina

Illustrations by Shanna and Joseph Morehouse of StarSite Media, LLC
Cover by Andrew Pinch of Collective, LLC

Dwaine's Why: Serving Leaders and Managers[1]

[1] Serving is helping, responding, anticipating, and encouraging with full attention to another's best interests.

To

Albie and Helen Pearson

encouragers, mentors, friends

CONTENTS

INTRODUCTION

Adopting a new methodology requires discipline. Those who grow and excel can force themselves to adjust old ways and adapt to new ways. This capacity for adapting to change and pursuing lifelong learning is a huge contributor to their successes.

The illusion of "freedom" with free-wheeling and haphazard approaches to leadership and management is intoxicating and often a harsh drug to overcome. The methodology and concepts in this book and the related online tools help you overcome the pitfalls and, in many cases, avoid some completely.

It is assumed readers have a successful organization or are developing and growing one. They recognize it is time to become more leaders and less day to day supervisors. Great success may have been achieved to this point with diligent focus on creating great products and/or services, delivery mechanisms, and attention to customers.

The next phases of an early-stage, emerging-growth company require the leadership and management team to build a full-dimensioned business around its products and/or services in order for it to flourish. There must be a vision for the whole business as it is and how it is to operate as it evolves.

In writing this book I hope I have maintained the truth of this four-hundred-year-old quote from the world's reputed most famous avid reader.

There is no book so bad...
that it does not have
something good in it.

—*Miguel de Cervantes Saavedra*, Don Quixote

Special Note: There are short summaries at the end of each chapter to make it easier for those who like to skim before they decide to read.

*If I had asked people
what they wanted,
they would have said
faster horses.*

—*Henry Ford, founder of Ford Motor Company*

WHAT IS NEEDED?

It's Time

This book introduces a methodology that provides structure and discipline to leadership and management of an organization's top level. Small and midsize organizations have rarely implemented this.

The top level of an organization encompasses all the activities between the principal leader and the management team. Out of it come the guidelines and principles used to create operating consistency between and within the functional parts of the organization.

A focus is needed on the big parts and the use of online tools to make their implementation easier. The big parts are explained in this book and are referred to in other books in this series. The online tools can be used at the website: www.Zynity.com. All of this is done explicitly for small and midsize organizations from ten to one thousand employees.

Small and midsize businesses can use another advocate, and I'm thankful to be one of them. These businesses bring great value to the United States as well as around the world. Their impact in numbers and reach are indisputable. Consider that in the United States, there are twenty-eight million small and midsize businesses that provide 60 percent of the jobs. They are an important force. Small is really big.

* * *

Small and midsize businesses are an important force

* * *

There is a huge need to help more small and midsize businesses survive and thrive. The first five years of a new company are pivotal and difficult. According to the Small Business Administration (SBA), **25** percent fail in their first year and **55** percent fail in the first five years. These statistics have been essentially the same for a few decades.

Many issues aggravate these results. A dominant missing ingredient is a *structured attention to leading and managing the top level* of the organization. A sales department may get disciplined by using processes and online tools. An operations department may get disciplined through the use of processes and online tools. An engineering department may get disciplined through the use of processes and online tools. The processes and online tools for the functional departments of an organization are developed to establish consistent steps—to get the same results in the same way over and over again.

* * *

Top level needs structured attention

* * *

The top level is often forgotten. Processes and online tools establish a disciplined and focused leadership and management dimension for the top level of these important organizations. However, the need for processes and online tools for the top level of an organization is different than the operating levels. Processes at the operating levels guide repetitive behavior. At the top level, processes establish an infrastructure that allows for doing new and different things in innovative ways within a defined structure that fit within the boundaries and parameters of the organization.

What prevents development of a focused, overt, and deliberate top level leadership and management system? A common reason appears to be that those who start an organization from the ground up get stuck in the lower levels of the organization in the building process and often never get out.

They don't escape for many reasons, but the one we address in this book is that they may not know exactly how to get out. This book presents an easy-to-implement way to lead and manage the top level. It combines the use of simple methodologies and online tools.

All professionals must do new things in new ways to progress. New things come with new concepts, new views, new expectations, and with deliberate "drills." Drills help them learn to turn all this newness into improved behaviors and greater results. Drills are concise, focused, step-by-step things to do. They allow professionals to overcome old ways and adapt to new ways in a disciplined manner until the new ways are being done correctly and comfortably. The online tools provide the mechanisms in which the drills can be exercised.

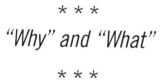

* * *

"Why" and "What"

* * *

This is deliberately both a "why" and a "what" book. It seems justifiable that we primarily focus on why and what in addressing a long-existing problem that needs much explanation and clarification. We bring a new perspective and a new solution. We also add new insight about the secondary problems this creates and the value solutions it will bring to those who implement our methods with the online tools.

The "how to" is more fully addressed in other resources we've developed and referenced in the book. The

Framework for Leading™ series of books, the courses, and the online tools at www.Zynity.com are devoted to explaining, illustrating, and guiding users to implement and become expert at using the methodology.

* * *

Organize leading and managing

* * *

The purpose of the methodology is to get leadership and management organized so it is done efficiently and effectively. This makes it easier and more engaging for everyone on the leadership and management team. Innovation is easier and more successful in an environment that is structured and focused.

Innovation is hard
because
solving problems people
didn't know they had
and
building something
no one needs
look identical at first.

— *Aaron Levie, CEO of Box*

LEADERS, MANAGERS, COACHES

This book is for leaders and managers who are growing organizations and are eager to improve how they lead and manage. This is not for everyone, but rather for the few who are actively and emotionally engaged in (not just talking about) accelerated ongoing improvement for themselves and their organizations.

It is also for coaches and consultants who want to get better connected with their clients to help them establish a focus on top-level leadership and management. Once the top level is implemented properly, then the necessary adjustments can be made more easily and effectively for the middle and operational levels.

* * *

Reasons to focus on the top level

* * *

The reasons that people begin to implement this methodology include

- wanting help in building and strengthening their own senior management team;

- preparing for a transfer of the business to the next generation;

- preparing an exit strategy;

- encouraging and accelerating profitability in their portfolio companies by angel and venture capital firms; and

- wanting to get organized and structured to lead and manage in a highly professional manner.

A highly professional manner means being

- disciplined;

- knowledgeable;

- structured;

- resilient;

- adaptable;

- coachable; and

- able to keep all the moving parts working in harmony.

The central part of the book is written as an exchange between a successful and aggressive entrepreneur who wants to get better and an executive consultant who works only with overachievers. A passionate desire to develop your own leadership and management system is necessary to enjoy this exchange.

The consultant introduces new concepts along with a set of online tools that establish the structure needed to adapt and make the required changes. The needed changes are about becoming a more polished professional as a leader and manager. Becoming more polished requires deliberate discipline. The result for the disciplined ones is a framework that incorporates the entrepreneur's individual strengths and style.

* * *

Get your garage organized

* * *

Begin with organizing the many things that are currently in use. This is similar to the process of putting in place all the scattered things in a cluttered garage, discarding or setting aside for the moment the unnecessary or unused items. Then the new things can be incorporated as needed. The online tools help organize each individual in the group while bringing them together as a leadership and management team.

The entrepreneur in this conversation has developed a successful organization and now needs to become more of a leader and less of a day-to-day supervisor. The organization has achieved great success with the focus primarily on creating great products and services and delivery mechanisms to customers.

The next phases of this emerging-growth company now require the entrepreneur to build a full-dimensioned business around its products and services in order for it to flourish. There must also be a vision for the whole business as it is and what it will become as it evolves.

Those building successful companies still have long hours, but it takes less effort, burden, and heartache. It also requires that they do some things differently than those who fail.

So, what must they do differently?

* * *

The conversation

* * *

The conversational format of the book highlights and illustrates the different concepts and points of view. This shows what businesses need to grow to their full potential and why the recommended concepts and steps will be of value.

The entrepreneur is Diane. She started her company three years ago. Its progress has been stellar. It's recently become profitable and cash-flow positive. Its strong operations get the necessities done in grand style. She thinks that most of the basics are solidly in place. The time has come to refocus on where the business needs to go and to develop a set of plans and operating infrastructure for getting it there. Her goals include "making happen" all that she perceives as the incredible potential of this business.

* * *

Success is a powerful motivator

* * *

She has certainly created and implemented great plans to get the business to this point. She senses it's time to adjust her operating infrastructure in advance of the anticipated growth. In the past, she figured out what to do when the time came. She is concerned the pattern of waiting to respond to needs as they arise will get her in trouble when the company is larger. Preparing in advance with the aid of someone who has done it before can help improve how she implements her present and future plans.

The coach/consultant is Cal. He has years of experience working with early-stage and start-up companies. He has also founded and built two of his own companies from the ground up. His engagement with all this is both personal and professional. His goal is to help his clients get to their proper places as quickly as possible, while learning about the things they'll need as their businesses grows quickly.

* * *

Learners win the prize

* * *

Cal engages best with those who are learners and are coachable. This doesn't mean they accept all that he says quickly and easily. It does mean that they listen, process, challenge, and then adapt their learning to apply it in a way that works best for them. The learning is not an academic focus, but it must be a practical-application focus. Through a process of application and assessment, they can learn concepts easily and thoroughly. However, without a process of immediate application, they tend to slip away from most, wasting their potentials.

Traditional academic learning is useful and necessary. Practical "street" learning is also useful and may be more necessary in building and growing a business. Applying what is learned is the most important aspect of the entire process. Applying it in relationship with others is necessary to build a strong "learning" organization.

* * *

Train, apply, and then refine

* * *

We've made the Train—Apply—Refine™ methodology foundational to learning and implementing the top-level leadership and management framework. It is illustrated as follows:

Personal Growth Cycle

Process:	Train ▶	Apply ▶	Refine
Principles:	Vocational	Experiential	Improve
Activities:	Do It	See the Value	Make It Better

It becomes a *personal growth cycle.* The process, principles, and activities create an easy-to-use cycle that increases the rate and levels of learning. Completing all the steps gives tangible experiences, which helps motivate ongoing improvement.

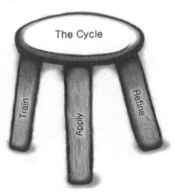

The process begins with an assessment. It can be taken at the www.Zynity.com website. Working through the assessment helps brings to light the missing items and those that are not as developed as they should be.

Diane completed the assessment on the website, as required by Cal. Her responses affirm that she is on path and a creative, tough, bright, resourceful, committed, and passionate learner.

Diane and Cal have agreed to a lunch meeting to share their interests. This allows both to determine if they can benefit and add value to each other. It must be an opportunity for a win-win.

*Never doubt that a small group
of thoughtful committed citizens
can change the world.
Indeed, it is the only thing
that ever has.*

*—Margaret Meade,
American cultural anthropologist*

1. LUNCH

Prepping for the future never ends

Greetings are cordial and friendly. This is their first meeting. Of course, both prepared by learning as much as possible about the other. Yes, they already had somewhat set their expectations, but there were also many things they wanted to explore more deeply.

After ordering lunch, Diane opens the get-to-it part of the conversation with the question, "So, why do you think I'm one who will benefit from the things you have to share?"

"A big reason would be that you appear to know how to ask great questions and get to the point," Cal replies, and they both chuckle. "I have a sense that you are very coachable, bright, and practical in your approach. You appear to have a self-initiated need to know, which should help us stay focused as we get to the tough places. However, it doesn't originate from a concern for failure but, rather, a need to succeed faster. The pinnacle goal still needs to be to develop a healthy profit, which is the fuel for all the other initiatives and needed results. I also believe you have a commitment to growth, balanced with a sincere attention to the details."

Diane asks, "Why is all that important?"

"Your results and history demonstrate that you are an aggressive competitor. Your personal demeanor in our first minutes of greeting suggests that you can stay the course, and even though you may become discouraged from time to time, you will not give in."

"I think that's an accurate assessment of me. But what do you mean about my demeanor?"

* * *

Aggressive is good

* * *

Cal replies, "You are clearly aggressive with all you've accomplished, but you're not abrasive. Sometimes people become like porcupines in order to express their aggressiveness. Those people lack confidence in some parts of who they are. However, aggressive people who are engaging give off warmth that expresses their confidence in their being. I don't mean to imply they're fully satisfied with themselves. They're convinced they're on a path to be better tomorrow and take comfort and pride in that."

"OK," Diane replies. "I'll accept all that as accurate as well as complimentary. We'll see how well I do relative to all this as we progress. I guess we both agree that I have a need to get a broader perspective of my business and put some new things in place if I'm to grow it beyond where it is today. I want to hear more details about that."

"So why have you agreed to meet with me? How do you think I might be of help to you?" asks Cal.

Diane replies, "I do want to grow my company quickly, but also correctly. There are many opportunities in our pipeline. I want to take full advantage of them. I also don't want to miss the window or falter in the process."

"I think I can be of help in that."

"I think you can, too. I want to have great plans. I also want to have a balanced way of leading and managing the company as it grows quickly. Your proposal of a top-level leading and managing framework with online tools intrigues me. I like the promise: you can help me and my management team make certain we give attention to the new things without losing attention to the daily things. I also want to make sure we're not just building a bureaucracy. I would like to qualify today that we'll deal properly with these concerns. Can you deliver on these promises?"

"I can," Cal says, "Before we get into the next details, let me ask another question. Do you want to distinguish yourself as a leader with your intelligence, strong personality, and character? Or do you want to also add to the description such features as organized, professional, thoughtful, and great at helping others grow in their leadership and management roles?"

Diane says, "Of course I want to add those characteristics and, to a certain extent, I already have."

"I think you have as well," Cal says. "But, we will take all that to new levels and capacities. It will become even more pronounced in how you lead and manage. I want to elaborate on a couple of points about being a leader. There are two dominant characteristics to which we need to add a third. The diagram is like this."

Cal pulls a diagram from a file folder to share with Diane.

Presence	&	**Personality**	&	**System**
Selling		Teaching		Organizing

"You can see that to the dominant characteristics of presence and personality, we need to add system. In the second row, you can see that when people are in selling or teaching mode, they rely on their personal presence and personality. With system added, it is like a three-legged stool. The organization gives the stability and fullness required to make a solid foundation for leadership and management. System is a necessary ingredient. This allows people to inspire others and facilitates their behaviors with direction and establishing a proper environment."

Cal shows Diane another diagram.

"I want to assure you that all this is not about building a bureaucracy. It's about building a system in which one can manage the complexity required to effectively grow a successful and efficient enterprise. The order and control it establishes does not require the 'controlling' of people. It gives individuals greater freedom to determine what they must do to add value at all times. It also builds your transparency. This adds to your warmth and their perception of your competency.

"We will develop together the next levels of details about what needs to be added to you, your team, and your company. Also, I want to make sure that you know this will be done over an extended period. It doesn't happen in a day. We incorporate the next things only when you and your team are ready for them. We pay careful attention to assuring the daily details do not get left out in this process.

"Please remember that the things we discuss today at lunch will be at a high level, and we'll get into more depth in the next sessions. This information is like the introductory session of a much longer course with its own body of knowledge. Even when we begin implementing the concepts and tools, we'll start at a beginning level, and then migrate to the greater depth and breadth of the topics in a manner and schedule acceptable to you and your team.

"Sometimes I may get too much in the weeds about a topic, but I'll do my best to stay high level. It will also be necessary to do some drilling into details to demonstrate the required processes. We'll just agree to flag that sort of thing in our exchanges."

* * *

Never shortchange the details

* * *

Cal says, "I do think it helps us establish a shared sense that even though we're going to focus primarily on high-level topics, the details are always necessary. It has been demonstrated many times that details get attended to better in well-ordered environments. Our general theme is that too many leaders too often get stuck in the details without establishing proper attention to the top-level needs of their organizations."

"Can you give me a clear example of one of the key things I'll get from this that benefits me and all those in my company?" asks Diane.

"I'll offer this. A few months into this, you'll have a heightened sense that others on your leadership and management team 'know where you're coming from.' Their sense of your predictability builds stability and an increased appreciation of your integrity. This adds to their trust of you and your transparency."

* * *

Systems help establish trust

* * *

"Please explain a bit further," Diane says.

"Your team will understand the system with which you lead and manage. They'll understand where you're headed with the big issues. They'll understand how and why you select initiatives. They will have collaborated in your process of developing implementation strategies. They will be in the loop at all times. This will give them a greater sense of peace.

"They'll understand, and it will be your shared system. They'll use the system and tools for their areas in the same way you use the system and tools. You'll be more predictable in the foundational issues of how you lead and make decisions. This is essential for you to build trust with your team."

* * *

Systems evolve

* * *

"The system you will evolve with these methodologies and online tools will grow over time and will fit within the daily activities," Cal says. "The system keeps all content organized so that the entire team has access to the same content. It doesn't tell anyone what content to use or how to use it. They just get better at using it in a common and cohesive manner. Everyone learns and collaborates in applying all this so that the team grows together, not apart. This creates better consistency and helps everyone improve and change without losing the good of yesterday."

"So it doesn't mean we have to throw away or forget all we currently know and do?" Diane teases.

Cal responds, "No, but it does mean you'll learn new things. It also means you may use some of the things you already know and do in different ways. You will have and use a defined system. The team will understand it and help evolve it. Members of the team will have a sense of ownership as they will see their individual contributions and those of others while using them. They will know how to work within the system, and they will know how to work the system."

Diane says, "So we build the system in this process. It's the system we continue to improve and we talk about it specifically."

"Yes and the difference is this. If I now ask you if you have a documented and defined system for leading and managing your business, you would answer 'no'. We begin with helping you develop and document it in a simple way. Then it grows as needed. It is a specific initiative to do this, and the whole team knows when it is being worked on.

"The impact on your team and their sense of being a part of it will transform how they do all of their activities and how they think about the company. This becomes a key mark of the organization's professionalism. It also becomes a key mark of making you a more predictable leader, as they will know the environment that shapes you. This encourages the team and gives them confidence to contribute better as they know the environment. The things they learn in this process will have been available to only a few, if any, in other places where they've worked. These will be transferable to everything the team does for their careers, and they will benefit greatly.

"I want to emphasize that these are more vocational and practical activities than academic exercises. You will learn a number of things learned along the way, but the focus is on applying them in the daily activities of your company. After people apply the new things, it's easier for them to expand their understanding and use of the principles and concepts that go along with these practical applications. The methodology we develop and employ is Train—Apply—Learn™ rather than learn about something, and then hope for an opportunity to apply it someday. It is learning to make it useful for the sake of immediate and longer-term improvement in how the company does business."

Summary

Diane and her team have already accomplished many wonderful things. The path to be better and grow is often more complicated than anticipated. A passionate desire and commitment to make new things happen is essential. It is paramount that one is coachable and pliable, both intellectually and emotionally. The implementation and ongoing development of the leadership and management system will transform the operating infrastructure of the company as well as the lives of everyone in it.

Life must have meaning, verve, substance, and power. It must be nurtured in an environment that is stimulating, safe, and conducive to adventure. One must have assurance that those around them are committed to them and to their shared reasons for being.

We build
too many walls
and
not enough bridges.

—*Isaac Newton*

2. TOP LEVEL

Every ship needs a bridge for the captain

Cal continues, "The main issue is around the need to have a top-level leadership and management system that serves as a platform from which to guide the ship. I hope you don't mind the analogy of a ship?"

"No, but I don't think my business is yet a ship. It's more of a speedboat that desires to be a fancy yacht," says Diane, and they both laugh.

"It may not be a ship yet, but for it to become one, we have to think of it as one and know that we are growing into our image of the future. Think of it as a ship with a crew. The crew is your current team. All the things that happen on your ship occur within its confines. For a ship to travel, it needs an engine, a hull (or body), a crew, and a place with controls to allow the skipper to guide it. The place is the bridge. It is at a high vantage point with windows to see all that is around the ship.

"In it is the equipment and controls of all kinds that aid in guiding the ship and communicating with the crew. Someone going up from the hull or engine room is 'going up top.' The bridge is the top level. I want to help you build a fully equipped bridge, and, together, we'll learn how to steer your ship and communicate with your crew.

"Let me show you a couple of diagrams to put this into business terms. This first one is a simple and traditional organizational chart. Not all organizations have all these parts staffed with separate people. Some organizations may have only a few of these boxes, but the activities in the boxes are required in most companies. The thing to see in this diagram is that the functional activities are the primary focus of the lead person. This is probably true in your current environment."

Cal looks through his file for a third diagram.

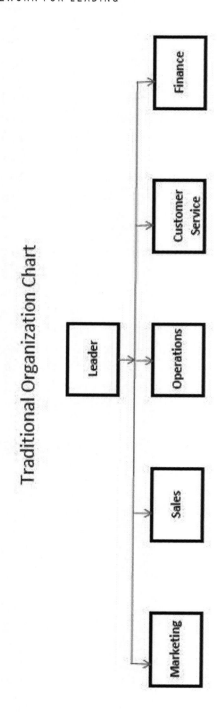

Traditional Organization Chart

"The chart shows the functional parts of the organization connected to the leader. Leaders spend most of their time helping and guiding each of the managers of these functional parts. A key goal is to make sure the managers do their parts in a way that works best for the whole organization."

"Isn't that the basic nature of the leadership role?" asks Diane.

"Yes, to an extent, but it's not all they should be doing. In too many cases, they get caught up in the business of each functional part and fail to spend the time creating a top-level focus," replies Cal.

"What kind of problems does that create for the company?" asks Diane.

* * *

Dependence versus independence

* * *

"One of the worst side effects is that the management team becomes too dependent on the principal leader. The more intensely the leader engages with each functional part, the more dependent each one becomes. Also, there is a tendency for leaders to emphasize their particular area(s) of strength and further weaken the team. The team members become like baby birds in a nest, waiting to be fed, rather than independent and doing as much as they should on their own.

Cal continues, "But if the leader encourages them to become more independent, they grow personally by assuming their own sense of autonomy. The leader must have a top-level focus and share overall leadership as well as delegate real leadership to the team in their functional areas. This must include the right to make mistakes without the risk of humiliation."

"What is a top-level focus to you, Cal?"

"Let me begin by explaining what I think it isn't. What if the ship's captain never left the engine room or came up top? I think this occurs far too often. Founders begin their businesses from the engine room and don't often get to the top or ever build a fully developed bridge. Nor do they learn to use the capabilities of a bridge properly. It requires building the bridge correctly and then transitioning so that the right balance and connection between up top and the engine room are established. The larger the business, the less time is required in the engine room. Weaning away from the engine room is hard without help.

"I think that in your business, you have a stairway to the bridge. You even have part of your bridge in place. Together, we can add some new equipment and increase your capacity to use it all better. Let me show you another diagram, and then we can talk about top-level focus from a common ground."

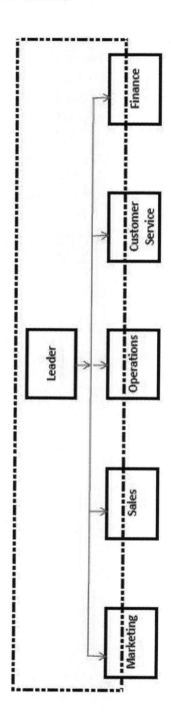

Top-Level Leading and Managing

* * *

The dotted-line box

* * *

Cal continues. "Inside the dotted-line box is the 'bridge' for the business. It is essential that leaders, in addition to being helpful inside the individual functional parts, have identified what they should be doing inside the dotted-line box."

"What things need to be done inside the dotted-line box?" asks Diane.

"Let me begin by highlighting that the dotted line cuts through each of the functional parts—but only their top thirds. There is nothing significant or rigid about the top third. It just conveys that there are things in the box that should have equal impact across all the functional parts. So the question is, what do we need to do at the top to provide a consistent and coordinated set of behaviors between the parts? The parts must know how to work together along certain principles and thoughts, even without the leader being present to remind them.

"There is a presumed set of 'leader' principles and thoughts that are useful for all parts. Unless they are documented and discussed on an ongoing basis, there may be gaps or inconsistencies so that they are not used uniformly throughout the organization. The gaps and inconsistencies are where dissonace and dysfunction for the organization are seeded and grown."

"What would be examples of thoughts and principles needed at this top level?" asks Diane.

"May I just give you a brief answer for now as I have a plan for later in the conversation for us to get into more detail?"

"Of course."

Cal says, "It may be different for each organization, but the list should include doing the right things, such as strategies and goals; connecting the management team; having a purpose; building a culture; having a customer focus; and measuring success. I call these 'big parts,' and we'll talk in more detail about them later. For example, the right things for the whole organization may be different from the right things for an individual, functional part. Each part has its own right things. However, they must be done in concert with the other parts as well as with the whole."

* * *

Document right things for each part

* * *

"The whole organization needs to express its own right things in documented form. It is your role to establish and maintain clarity about the right things for the whole organization. This makes it possible for others to better understand them and to include them in all that they are doing as well. Proper documentation and sharing helps each part do its portion much better. It makes leading and managing easier, more efficient, and more effective for all the leaders and managers."

Diane says, "This may be a good time to tell you that our team enjoyed completing the assessment survey. They were surprised to find that we have so much to do to get to where we want to be in implementing these big parts. Each part had different, but similar, ratings. The team was also surprised to find that we are not as deliberate as we all know we need to be in these areas. Is that common?"

"Yes, it's common for teams to find they haven't really clarified where they stand in their thinking and what they're doing around these not so obvious issues," Cal says.

"How do you feel about how our team rated us in the assessment?" Diane asks.

"If you're asking for me to share how you compare with other similar organizations, I can say that you have a great start in doing all this better. Assessments fall everywhere in the spectrum for each of the big parts and the related items. It's up to you and your team to take on the commitment to get better assessmments based on your own standards and expectations."

* * *

Assess regularly to monitor progress

* * *

"What is important is to keep reassessing, first on a monthly basis for six months, and then quarterly on an ongoing basis. This type of insight provides awareness and encouragement. It becomes another scoreboard to 'see how you're doing' that goes beyond just 'feeling how you're doing' based on anecdotes and the freshness of major incidents."

* * *

Strategy versus implementation

* * *

"So, is this about strategy or implementation?" Diane asks.

"Both. An idea is often a statement about what you want to accomplish. Strategy is usually a developed form of how to make an idea happen. Strategies provide a reason and a pathway to getting things done more efficiently. Creating simple and direct strategies provides a distinct advantage in implementation. 'Winging it' almost always creates disasters that cause havoc down the road.

"Ideas are a dime a dozen unless they are implemented correctly. This includes full business models and also key initiatives that add to an existing business model. We set the course or strategy from the top level, but we get there by keeping the engine running properly and steering in the right direction at all times. The top-level concepts and tools provide the guidance for doing all this properly."

Summary

It is esssential to establish a top-level leadership and management methodology and making it central to how the organization works. Organizations often discover that they are not doing as well in some important areas as they thought they were and know that they should be. With the methodology in place, the organization will create and maintain an environment in which all the parts together in harmony. The focus will be on right things and doing them in the right way.

*Ideas
without action
are worthless.*

—*Harvey Mackay, businessman, author,
and syndicated columnist*

3. IDEAS ARE A DIME A DOZEN

Strategies Pave the Way to Make Ideas Happen

Diane says, "So, my business began with an idea and a set of connected thoughts to form a business model. We have gotten this far by developing and implementing strategies to get all the things done that need to get done."

"Precisely," Cal replies.

"So, is the purpose of this exchange for us to make sure we think about what we are doing at the conceptual level?" Diane says.

"And what else comes to mind?"

"I'm thinking that we are establishing our common vocabulary with which we'll learn to more carefully express what we need to share and understand."

"Correct. All professional people, including those within small and specialized teams, tend to create their own private lexicon. It becomes one of the key strands that weave them tightly together," Cal says.

"This could get a bit tedious. Is it necessary, or is it just fun for you?" Diane asks.

"It's both. This top level thinking is its own world, and most do not engage it well. They have loose understandings that limit later progress and slow progress even in the early stages. Let me share an example. I worked with a company from the idea stage. A brother-in-law had an idea to add new capabilities to a physical-therapy table.

"The new product solved two problems. One was that physical therapists experienced injuries by lifting patients. The next was that a second physical therapist was often required to help give patients confidence that they would not be injured in their therapies. When I asked the founders to describe their business, they explained it by amplifying the new product. They thought their business *was* the product."

* * *

A product or a business

* * *

3. IDEAS ARE A DIME A DOZEN | 27

"When I asked if they intended to have only one product, they paused, and quickly agreed that there should be more than one. From that moment, their vision of the company evolved into a set of many products/services and not just a single one. We talked about their business as being something quite different from, and yet including, their product. The business has its own life and facets separate from its products and/or services.

"If they had not made this distinction, they would have focused all their energy and resources on the product/service and given less attention to building the overall business needed to develop, manufacture, sell, and service the envisioned set of products/services and its customers. Their expanded view transformed them and the company.

"What happens when the distinction is not made? The other dimensions or facets of the business don't get the development attention needed. They remain underdeveloped. Such things as accounting, customers, human resources, and the top level don't get fully implemented. The results will not be good, if the business grows and the leaders are thinking only or mostly about the product. It helps to understand as soon as possible that the product is just one distinct part of the business and behave accordingly. The other parts of the business that produce and distribute the product are also distinct parts of the whole entity and also deserve focused attention."

"Aren't they just two different parts of the same thing?" Diane asks.

"Of course, we could say yes and leave it at that, but this distinction is essential if you want to grow your business so that it operates in a highly professional manner. An example would be that if we wanted to have a single location of a restaurant. The ownership team could evolve and do their parts daily, and we could make it work really well. If the ownership wants to have more than one location and yet serve the same quality meals, then they have to build the business so that others can do it all as they would. This allows it to become a business that can be replicated in many locations."

* * *

Documented processes are essential

* * *

"If an organization decides to franchise, it takes an even more formalized process of operations, and the individual units become even more distinct from the franchisor business. The franchisor is very distinct from the franchise locations. Franchise organizations have to build a top level in order to be a franchise. Other organizations are not forced to, so they evolve with the businesses as extensions of the products, rather than as separate entities within which the products evolve."

Diane says, "Will you tie this back to the part of our discussion where idea, strategy, and implementation are three separate concepts? I want to make sure I'm tracking with you here. May I summarize all this in my way?"

"That would be great."

Diane continues, "An idea is the thought or set of thoughts about a product or service that people will pay for. A set of strategies are needed to develop the product or service. A different set of strategies is used to build a business to provide the product or services. It is in implementing the strategies that the right things are done, and the business grows."

Cal says, "I agree with all that."

* * *

Diane gets it

* * *

Diane says, "A mistake that leaders often make is that they don't fully develop the business dimension of all this. The product or service is done so well that it creates a life of its own to an acceptable level of success. But if the business dimension doesn't get its own attention and development, the enterprise will begin to fray. The business makes it so hard to deliver the product or service that it all becomes less fun.

"You equate this condition to when the ship engine and its hull have grown so big that it becomes difficult to keep it on a growth trend. The bridge or business dimension (the top level) doesn't exist to the extent needed. This is where many businesses stall. Do I have this right?"

"Perfectly."

"OK, what's next?"

"Where do you think your business is in this sketchily drawn scenario?"

"Our products and the services around them are very good. I do need to learn more about this bridge, or top level. We have some of it in place, but we can do it better. That's where we need help. We have a chance to grow this really big, and we need that business-growth infrastructure to be as good as our products and customer service."

Summary

Great ideas without a proper business model, strategies, and keen discipline to implement them create little value. Ideas of marginal consequence with a proper business model and excellent implementation will likely create great value. Implementation is just as, or more, important than ideas.

*It starts
with this obsession
for every individual
and organization
to do more
and be more.*

—Satya Nadella, CEO of Microsoft

4. MORE IS NOT ENOUGH

Greatness is in the eye of the holder

Cal says, "You are personally committed to a greatness that you probably haven't, as yet, even accurately defined for yourself. I admire that immensely. It's necessary for you to develop your organization to its full potential. Time will reveal whether you just want it or if you will have it.

"Probably no need to warn you, but I will. The quest for greatness is ongoing. More and better is a never-ending pursuit. The one pursuing greatness sees it differently than the one who observes it. Those who get recognized by others capture the gold. They represent greatness. They now see it in a whole new way.

"Greatness is a show of accomplishment. It is attained by doing big things through execution of the smallest details in an exceptional manner. The separation between a silver and gold medal at the Olympics is a very small measurement and is created by attention to detail. The separation between success and failure in an organization is a very small measurement and is created by attention to detail.

"It becomes another case of the importance of the "and". The big things must be executed extremely well *and* the details must be executed extremely well. This is especially true in leading and managing."

* * *

It's about the "and"

* * *

"A big difference in the world of organizations is that many leaders and managers are very good at executing the smallest details, but they're not always able to execute the big things extremely well. I hope to convince you that the most noticeable missing piece in most organizations is the structure for executing the leading and managing.

"Doing the big things well makes it possible to give the added attention needed to do the smallest details. When the big things are not being done extremely well, small details can't keep the overall organization from running aground, sinking, or falling off a cliff. Think of each musician playing each note beautifully in harmony with the other musicians while the Titanic sank. The result was no matter how well they played they couldn't save the ship or the people."

Diane says, a bit defensively, "I think we do many of the big things fairly well."

"I'm sure you do," Cal says.

Diane continues, "We would not have had as much progress and success as we have if we did not do the big things really well."

"I agree," Cal says. "And certainly when compared to others you've seen come and go with their businesses and ideas."

"So maybe I need you to put all this in a different context for me," Diane suggests.

"Yes, let me do that," Cal says. "Let me share a personal incident that gave me an important perspective on learning at the higher levels?"

* * *

The Tom Anton incident

* * *

"It's a golf story," Cal says.

"That's OK. I've played golf since I was very young."

Cal says, "OK, so you will understand this even better. I started playing golf when I was forty. Because I had resources, I could take lessons and I'm a learner so I follow advice. The primary advice was to take lessons, practice what I was taught—a lot, and to play only occasionally so I wouldn't pick up bad habits. After three years of following that advice and being a little obsessive, I got my handicap index down to a five."

Diane says, "That's very good, considering the average index is around an eighteen."

"Yes, it was very good, but I wasn't satisfied. I felt I could get better. I found a golf coach, Tom Anton, whose student had won the tour qualifying school for the PGA Tour the prior year, and I asked him to be my coach. I played a round of golf with him to let him see my game. Afterward, we went to lunch to talk about our plan.

"I said, 'Well, Tom, will you take me on as a student?'

"'Of course, I will, he said. 'What's your objective?'

"'I want to get my index down so that I play at scratch with a zero index,' I replied.

"'That's a big goal, Cal.'

"'Can I do it?' I asked.

"'I think you can, but it will take a lot of work.'

"I pulled a yellow three-by-five card from my left pocket and shoved it over to Tom for him to read. It contained a list of the eight parts of the game I was working on and the number of hours I worked on each during the week. Tom read through the list carefully.

"He lifted his eyes from the card and said, 'I've never seen a list like this from an amateur before. You are really organized in your thinking. And, you shot a seventy-four out there today from the back plates on a very tough course. So I've seen you in action.'

"With great expectation, I said, 'well, what do you think?'

"Tom paused for a moment. "You're a really good athlete and you work hard, or you wouldn't play at the level you do. I would go anywhere with you as a partner at your five index. But if you want to get to a zero index, you have a whole bunch to learn.'"

* * *

Surprised at much to learn

* * *

"I was shocked to hear I had a whole bunch to learn," Cal said. "I expected him to say a little polish here with my game and a little polish there, and I could quickly get to a zero index."

"Why did you think it would be easy and take a short time?" Diane asks.

"I had heard from so many people how good I was and how close I was, and so I thought it would be quick and easy," Cal responds, "Back to the story.

"Tom could see the disappointment in my face. But he didn't want to lead me on. He shared that I would have to spend twice as much time as I had on my yellow card, and, so, I would have to give up my business.

"And he said, 'As a five, you know a great deal about golf, but as to what it takes to be zero, you don't know anything. I saw your targets out there today. You don't know how to manage your way around a course. If I had stopped you at various times to ask you what you were thinking, I know you wouldn't say you were thinking about the right things. Even though you created fairly good results today, I know you can't get to the next level by thinking the way you currently think.'"

* * *

New things require new thinking

* * *

"'It takes a whole new way of doing and thinking about things,' Tommy continued. 'You can get there, but it will take time, and you'll have to adopt new thinking and adapt to new ways of doing things. The advantage is that you don't have years of bad habits to overcome, but it will take a lot more time. Are you ready to sell your business and go full time into getting a zero index? There are a lot of fun things you can do competing in tournaments, but it will be a big sacrifice for you.'

"I asked, 'How long will it take?'

"Tom replied, 'It will take at least three years or more, and it's still not guaranteed.'

"I was completely deflated. I was not ready to give up my business. I told Tom I would think about it and get back to him."

"So, you didn't go forth with it?"

"No, I didn't. Tommy became my regular golf instructor, and I made some progress, but the thought of a zero index was no longer in my mind. If I wanted to retire from my business and make a career of golf, I would have done it."

Diane asks, "Did you think you really couldn't do it, or was the love of your business just more important?"

"That's a great question. My reality was that I could have sold my business and retired, but doing it for a golf index seemed frivolous. However, it also occurred to me that if I made this bold move, and I failed at getting to zero, that would be the worst of all possible outcomes."

"So, a bit of fear of failure was in the picture as well?" Diane says.

"You're right," Cal says.

* * *

Fear of failure versus prudence

* * *

"Was this a made-up story or a real-life incident?"

"It was a real-life incident and there is a real-life Tom Anton who I still admire greatly," Cal says.

"So why did you share this story with me? What are the life lessons for me and my circumstances?"

"I hoped you'd ask. Being as direct as I can be, let me share these two points. Point one: Getting to a new level of capability requires a lot of hard work and doing things differently than you currently do. Point two: This is still optional for you, but in your case, we are talking about your current chosen profession which is entrepreneur, executive, business leader, and teacher of others."

* * *

New things in new ways

* * *

"We are not asking you to give up your business and retire, but rather give up your sense of comfort and pay the price of doing new things in new ways so that you can become a more fully equipped leader and manager."

Diane says, "You don't really think I have an option, do you? Or do you think I'm not willing to work hard enough? Which is it?"

"What's your decision?"

"I'm not ready to make a decision yet about your methodology but I've already made my decision to. I don't have enough information about your stuff. I need to determine if what you have to offer will get me to a zero index from my current five. I think your story frames for me what you will ask of me and also what your assessment is of me."

"What is my assessment of you?" Cal replies. "I'm not fully sure of that yet."

"Are you willing to share your best guess at the moment?" asks Diane.

"Certainly, I will. In the example of golf, I think you're a solid ten index. I think we can get you to a five in a year or so, and then get you on a path to zero, which will take another couple of years. It's a big journey, and it will pay off in multiples. It's a journey that will have its ups and downs, but with a great upward trend along with notable successes."

"So you have confidence in me?"

"Yes, I do. But even more important, I know you have confidence in you, and you're not afraid of hard or smart work."

Diane asks, "Why should I do this?"

"What do you think 'this' is?" Cal asks.

"Implement and learn to use a more structured leading and managing system," she replies.

"That is correct," Cal says. "But, it is primarily for the top-level part of the organization. You likely already have some structure and a number of systems in place for the middle and lower parts of your organization. With this methodology we add a single, overarching system to the top level."

"What should I expect this to do for me and the company?" asks Diane.

* * *
Why do this?
* * *

"First, it will build in a foundation for growing and scaling your business that is solid and identifiable. You will know it, as will the others, and you'll know when you are evolving it. Second, it will make work life easier and more fun for the whole team. Third, productivity will improve throughout the organization. Fourth, it will help individuals develop so they grow in capability, ability, and confidence. Fifth, it will make each of you more predictable (not rigid) in your actions. You will take actions within a framework that each knows about and understands.

"These last four accomplishments add value to all the stakeholders and all of their connected parties. Each member's influence impacts that person's big part of the world. The ripple effects go far beyond just your company. You become a learning and knowledge building company in which everyone is respected and acknowledged for whom they are and what they contribute."

"How much time will all this take, and what is the expected pain level for everyone?" asks Diane.

* * *

Transition time is important

* * *

"The transition time for implementing the full system begins with only one hour per week per member. Then, as tools are adopted and behaviors change, it takes a bit more time, but it becomes a part of normal activities so it is not an added factor. Adding new tools or upgrading to a more advanced version of a tool should generally be restricted to one hour or less per week for a two to three week learning period. The full amount of calendar time will depend on how quickly the team adopts the tools and adapts to their use. My experience suggests it takes six to eighteen months. It all depends on you and your team."

Diane asks, "So, what are the big things you feel I need to learn and know to apply in order to become a five or zero index as a business owner and leader? You have to tell me more so I'll have enough information to make a decision to start this journey you speak of."

Summary

You must be a "more is never enough" type of person to get to your next level of capabilities. Shrinking from this by delaying is the same as avoiding it completely. Settling at any point is a decision that "enough is enough," and progress from there is usually quite little. You determine, to a great extent, your own capabilities, capacities, and destiny.

*The most valuable
of all talents
is that of never
using two words
when one will do.*

—*Thomas Jefferson*

5. TOP LEVEL COMMUNICATING

Start with headlines

Cal continues, "The first big thing is communicating. Expressing yourself with words and tone is half, and the other half is getting others to hear with accurate understanding. Style and techniques do matter. Verbal communication is different from written communicating. Communicating around an operating table is different from communicating with a race-car driver during a race. Likewise, communicating around leading and managing an organization requires its own ways.

"In all environments, communication begins with a clear understanding of what one is talking about. Imagine the front page or any page of a newspaper, with all the normal type set in regular columns, but there are no headlines for the various articles. Imagine that each story begins with the first paragraph, and then rattles along. Often it would take a paragraph or two to fully grasp what the story is about."

* * *

News article-type headlines

* * *

"Thankfully, all newspapers, and even most newsletters and e-mails, have headlines. The headline sets the context and makes the specific topic at hand clear. You can decide if want to know more about the topic, or you can scan right past. Simplicity and elegance should be used with the concept of headlines. Simplicity and elegance are not synonyms, but you can usually only get to elegance with a big measure of simplicity.

"Teaching all levels of leaders and manager to speak in headlines is important, and you should be great or at least very good at it before teaching others. Then, if needed, you can follow up with a concise opening short sentence or three-sentence paragraph. This skill is essential to lead and manage today. It teaches you how to conceptualize. This leads to expressing context and clear relevance of the information you need to convey."

"Why do you think this is so important?" asks Diane.

* * *

Clearly express relevance

* * *

"So much information is created today, and it helps people sort through what they should be reading. It helps focus direct attention to the right topic in its most succinct description. It forces those who are communicating to formulate the context of what they want to communicate. It stops them from starting their messages from a random place. The discipline is as important for those sharing messages as it is for those receiving them. We must help one another on both ends of the communicating process," Cal replies.

"Getting things done in an organization requires the exchange of information to cause something to happen that benefits the company in some way. Almost all action in an organization requires communication."

* * *

Executive speak is succinct

* * *

"Communication between individuals at the top level has impact throughout the organization. Each communication at all levels could be said to create impact or ripples of impact throughout the organization. Therefore, doing it well is a critical capability.

"It is considered right form to begin a presentation of information to a high-level executive in a larger organization with a concise statement. I'm labeling that a form of headline. It establishes focus, context, and purpose and puts the listener in a place of expectation and makes it easier to understand what the speaker is saying.

"When topics are important to the receivers, they will be more curious as to what will follow. The topics themselves may establish reasons for receivers to be curious.

"People in all levels of an organization often list communications as the number one problem or number one opportunity for improvement. If everyone learned to speak beginning with a headline, things would improve immediately. This adds a dimension of thinking before communicating. The thinking step helps you really focus on the message you want to convey (have the recipient grasp) and not just on what you want to say. It is an important discipline that takes a bit of learning and ongoing refining."

Diane asks, "When people complain about communications being a problem in their companies, what are they really talking about?"

Cal replies, "There are many things I'm sure, but the main ones center around the following areas. One, people often feel caught off-guard by the decisions made by others at the next level and their peers. Two, news comes late or after rumors have been in circulation so people feel out of the loop and disrespected. Three, notifications are simply unclear. Four, often only a few understand the reasons behind the decisions, and so others feel like they 'don't know where they came from.' And five, there is no forum in place for people to share the things that are going on in their areas that are not a part of weekly meetings.

"The last item is the one that stings the most and yet is expressed the least often. The weekly meeting topics usually cover only the visible and hot issues and opportunities, and the rest is treated as if they are not important for the group. Part of this is caused by sensitivity to length of meetings and not everything can be highlighted. The ones who handle their issues, without fanfare, do so without complaint, but others don't get the opportunity to recognize the value they create. My very rough calculation is that sixty percent of what people work hard at and create never gets recognized by their peers. Yes, those are their jobs, but getting recognition still helps immensely."

Diane asks, "How do you solve this, and recognize people for the things that happen in the shadows?"

"The tools and sharing of headlines list these 'shadow' issues, and people can make comments about each one. This may be only passing acknowledgment, but the owner of the issue knows that others see it on their lists. This allows people to have one hundred percent of their big issues recognized, and prevents them from being completely ignored.

"The kind of recognition statements that come from this are, 'I had no idea you had so many other things going on in your area,' and, 'Thank you for making that process better, as it will really help our area perform better as well.' All of this keeps everyone better informed, and everyone getting full acknowledgment for all that they are doing."

Summary

Communication in organizations should begin with a concise statement or headline of what is to follow. This prepares the listener and helps establish context. This forces the messenger to label the coming information exchange in a summary that helps focus the content. It aids hearing and understanding.

Sharing issues that are necessary, but not "newsworthy" helps everyone stay better attuned with all that is happening. Those things that get done in the shadows (out of the limelight) and are expected but not recognized often cause people to feel ignored and undervalued. This can be particularly frustrating when people are doing great work with great results in their shadow issues and struggling with their work on an issue that's in the limelight.

Simplicity
is the
ultimate
sophistication.

—*Leonardo da Vinci*

6. BIG PARTS AND TOOLS

Major dimensions and their impact

Cal continues, "Big parts are the major pieces that many organizations do not usually implement properly throughout the organization. They convey big ideas and have broad impact. There four big parts in an organization: strategies, customers, managing team, and measurements. Think of them as dimensions that influence each of the functional parts as well as the whole organization."

Cal showed Diane a diagram.

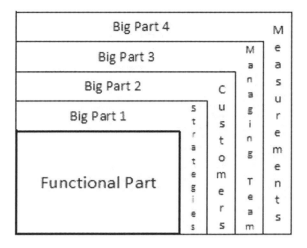

"A marketing department is an example of a functional part. Each big part is a dimension of each of the functional parts. The influence and impact of a big part is determined by the consistency with which it's implemented in each functional part and throughout the organization. We'll talk more about each of the big parts later. For the moment, we need to grasp the important concept of a big part being a 'big idea' that is a 'necessary ingredient' and its impact is woven throughout all functional areas.

"It must exist in a unique way within each functional area. It must also be guided by consistent general principles throughout the organization. In a sense, it is like the musical score for an orchestra. Each part has the same music but is directed to do different things at different times so the instruments fit together and create harmony within the whole. This encourages all members of the team to be conscientious about their roles, the concepts, and the details.

"This is a way to capture the host of moving parts in the complex and dynamic world of leading and managing and bring focus to them. They must be implemented within the dotted-line box in the organization chart I showed you earlier."

Cal pulls out the dotted-line diagram again.

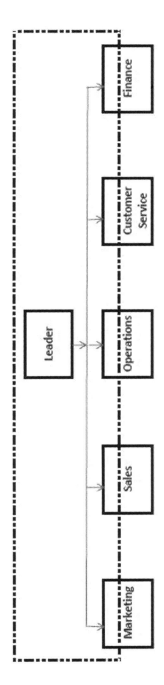

Top-Level Leading and Managing

"Leading and managing are not restricted to one dimension. No one thought or slogan or activity will make an organization function to its highest level. Many dimensions must be underway and active in the right ways for the right reasons in order to establish the harmony needed for effective and efficient operations.

"I call these dimensions big parts because they must be active in a consistent manner across all functional areas at all times. These are the layers or dimensions behind an org chart that bring breadth and depth to the organization. The principal leader and the leadership and management team must work together to ensure that this happens to establish symphony rather than cacophony. A cohesive framework built upon these big parts makes it easier and more effective. It is important to state that these can be implemented in different ways by different organizations. Each has its own style. But there must be a consistency of use within each organization so that the style is the same within each functional part of the company."

* * *

Simplify the complexity

* * *

"The purpose of a big part is to help establish simplicity in the midst of complexity. Organizations are complex. Addressing this complexity with big parts helps you interact with the organization's parts in their simplicity. Everything—what you do, how you do it, and why you do it—must be around the consideration of learning and evolving. Everyone must become learners and teachers. Big parts provide shortcuts to aid learning and evolving. The online tools guide the learning and add a vocational dimension to the process. There is a shared process with others, and the repetition reinforces the quality of applying what is learned. The digital engagement enhances retention.

"An important feature of all this is the need and ability to innovate. Innovation in all ways and at all levels is a key for success. Innovation is easier in an organization that has structure. Big parts add to the structure."

* * *

Innovation is paramount

* * *

"I need to introduce and clarify the use of the terms 'big part' (singular) and 'big parts' (plural), as they help us build clarity. 'Big part' isn't a term that is used broadly in the world of leading and managing. It's risky to start using a new term, but by the time we finish our lunch, I hope you'll find it useful."

* * *

Big Parts

* * *

"The principle of a big part is exactly what is needed to build a top level leading and managing system. The definition of a big part for our purposes covers the two thoughts of 'extent' and 'impact'. Each big part applies and contributes across the full breadth and depth of the organization. This is a key to establishing consistency between the functional parts so they have a much easier path for working together."

* * *

Make it easy for parts to work together

* * *

"Clarity of the big parts makes the structures of the functional parts and how they work together and are defined in a consistent way. And maybe most importantly, it provides a way to deal with complexity. These days of information deluge and limitless options demand a way to organize and simplify. This is not unlike a home's car garage with all sorts of things randomly stored in it, leaving no room for the car.

"The use of the big-parts concept provides a way to accomplish two things. First, it allows you to ignore all but the essentials, and, second, it helps organize all the scattered knowledge into its proper place for ready access. Yes, it also encourages throwing away many of the items that cause the clutter and confusion as they aren't used anyway."

* * *

Ignore distractions and streamline

* * *

"When the top level has all the big parts correctly implemented it connects more fluidly to the middle level of
the organization. This allows the midlevel to connect
properly to the operational level. The disciplines and
big parts of the top level, woven across all the functional
parts, encompass all levels as a matter of course.

"Each big part must be implemented in such a way that
the functional parts are bound together. Even though
they are separate parts, the consistency of the big parts
provides commonality. The organization can work
seamlessly when the functional parts are designed
to work together. Implementing the big parts makes
working together happen more easily.

"Big part also applies to the ability to see the 'big picture.' It designates a view of things from a broader perspective. Compare the illustration of one looking into
a tunnel from the entry point versus looking out of the
tunnel from the exit point. The broader view gives you
the ability to see the pieces of the landscape from a
different perspective.

"Instilling the ability to establish a big part view, as
needed, will help you avoid being lost in the forest for
the trees. One common observation from individuals growing organizations is that they would like their

teams to 'see it' from their eyes, but teaching others to do that is not always so easy."

* * *

Use of Online Tools

* * *

"Each big part has its own documentation and structure. You implement it using the online tools at the Zynity Leadership™ website. The tools allow you to keep the documentation current and accessible by all parties. This continuous and current updating keeps the top-level leadership and management capacity flexible and ready for the next stages of growth or changes in company direction.

"Use of the tools keeps the information current. It helps the organization stay ahead of the growth curve. It is also establishes an environment in which the team takes more ownership, contributes, and recognizes others as they extend their friendships and relationships as collaborators.

"If a company is growing, it needs to adjust its capacity for operations/production as well as its capacity for sales. Does it seem that the leading and managing system required for a two-million-dollar company would work for a twenty-million-dollar company?"

Diane responds, "Not likely. But what would be the differences?"

* * *

Growth is not easy

* * *

Cal answers, "The larger company requires a more formal infrastructure, including more documented processes, more people, and more departments. Think about the training required to make that happen correctly. The online tools allow easy expansion of the framework as needed. The documentation and mechanisms for sharing the information are already in use.

"Consider also that this means a one-million-dollar company can implement the framework for leading and managing the top level. It helps it grow at the various stages. It also helps it operate in a more organized way while it's still smaller. The online tools expand and have additional capabilities for the leading and managing in the same way that a CRM system expands its customer relationship management capacity with little adjustment. The discipline required to use the online tools when the company is smaller remains essentially the same when it becomes larger. This is what makes it an expandable and scalable platform."

Summary

Establishing the big parts and weaving them across and throughout the functional parts of an organization is essential to establish consistency. It also creates a guiding mechanism that gets the functional parts to work together better. This system can be implemented for small and midsize organizations with equal success. The sooner it is implemented in an organization's life cycle the sooner it will contribute to the organization's ability to grow and prosper.

The online tools serve as ways to develop and maintain a consistent set of thinking and behaving habits "drills" to assure that all the content is used properly. They become the key repositories of the content and pathways for sharing it between individuals. The online tools also establish a common way of sharing information that each individual understands. All of the management team learns to speak the same language and in the same style, and it's available to everyone at all times.

...leadership
is doing
the
right things.

—Peter F. Drucker, Essential Drucker:
Management, the Individual and Society

7. BIG PART 1: STRATEGIES

The start of leading and managing

Cal continues, "This big part defines what you want to happen and what it will take to let everyone know when it *has* happened. The other big parts bring the people in the organization together so that they can work together while providing ongoing feedback as to how to adjust the 'right things.' When I say 'right things,' what does that bring to your mind?"

Diane replies, "It implies making correct choices about strategies, priorities, business models, products/services, markets, funding, and determining other initiatives where the organization should spend its available resources with careful budgeting. It could also include such things as determining if there is the need for more financial resources and developing a plan to get them."

Cal begins, "Well said. I would add that right things require carefully constructed strategies in order to implement them properly. I'll use the term strategies as the overarching term for developing plans and schedules to do right things at the right time in the right way. Informally, I use the blanket term 'right things.'

"Getting focused so that the entire organization is working on the right things is a generally accepted starting place for leading. Defining the right things begins at the top level. This definitely fits in the area of the dotted-line box, don't you think?"

Diane responds, "I do, and most people consider this a high-level, or leadership, thing to do."

Cal continues, "A key part of this is setting in place broad perspective strategies and visions for the entire company and its various parts. Each functional part should have its own set of strategies, visions, and missions and a clear purpose that fits within the overall picture.

"Often, each group places this thinking in a document and gets attention in varying ways. Sometimes the strategic plans get stated clearly in a planning document but are often left out of the operational processes and midlevel strategies. The statement that planning is its own reward is true. However, planning that doesn't get implemented is not nearly as valuable as it could have been."

* * *

Plans should be implemented

* * *

"The concepts for this methodology include that planning gets done in meetings and is recorded in the online tools that are used daily. This assures that they are visible and implemented and in the scheduled time frame. There are many books and great teachings about visioning and strategies and the importance of being clever and creative with both. In the work we will do together, I'm more concerned about getting them done properly than in being awestruck with the idea associated with the role of being a visionary. I'm hoping to have you think more intensely and deliberately about distinguishing yourself as one who 'makes it happen.'"

* * *

Make it happen

* * *

"My hat is off to the ones who get it done. Business superstars such as Steve Jobs, Jeff Bezos, Larry Ellison, Tony Hsieh, Jack Welch, Bill Gates, Marc Benioff, and Mark Zuckerberg are all make-it-happen people. Yes, they may be visionaries but, their real mark is as 'get-it-doners.' They accomplish all this with ideas, strategies, and engaging people within a leadership and management system that keeps everyone focused and intensely engaged with doing right things in the right way."

Diane asks, "Why are you making such a point about getting it done when we're talking about the right things and choosing the right things? Isn't this the other side of doing right things?"

"You are correct. It's the other side, and I'm on a tangent here because often, even when leaders choose the right things, they don't focus properly to make them happen. So I'm returning to our discussion that ideas are a dime a dozen, but making sure it all happens is where you really attain greatness.

"So I'm just belaboring the point that the system is focused on making sure things get done. The ideas for right things come from your input into the online tools. The collaborative use of the tools provides the guidance and focus needed to do the right things in the right way.

"To this point we've talked about right things for the company as a whole. We also need to spend the same quality of focus to establish the right things for each of the functional parts. In this way, the parts become connected and support the whole. I have found that some companies develop strategies and right things for the parts, but they do it with less passion."

* * *

Each part has its own right things

* * *

"There is a general belief that if 'right things' are stated company-wide, then the parts will have all the direction they need to do their parts. Of course, this is not always true. The parts need the same level of passion and focus to define and follow through with their portions of the right things. This opens the door that allows the functional parts to more easily define how they are supposed to work with others to make the right things happen correctly. Managing is the set of activities required to get all the right things done in the right way at the right time to create the greatest value."

Cal shows Diane a simple diagram.

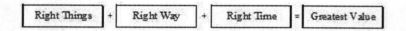

Diane says, "I agree with that, and we do a fairly good job of it. I'm interested to see how the tools help us do this better."

Cal replies, "I'm eager to see how it works for you also. It helps overcome what a common opiate for hard-charging and hardworking management teams in emerging companies. There seems to be an accepted belief that if I stay busy, good things will happen.

* * *

Stop to sharpen the axe

* * *

"If I'm not busy, I'm being lazy. However it's in this condition that the urgent drives attention away from the essential. I like the quote attributed to Abraham Lincoln, 'Give me six hours to chop down a tree, and I will spend the first four sharpening the axe.'

Cal continues, "That helps me keep the perspective that it is essential to think about what you're going to do before getting busy doing it. The thinking and planning help you do it better, and then you have to redo it less often."

Diane says, "I definitely agree with that. It's much better to do things right the first time."

"But I am, as are others, highly motivated by the 'greater good' purpose of what I'm doing. How what I do benefits others and/or the world at large is of extreme importance."

* * *

Love of purpose creates passion

* * *

Cal continues, "It is generally accepted that passion is an ingredient in all exceptionally motivated people. The organization's purpose or reason for being starts the pathway toward passion. Passion begets commitment and intensity, which are necessary to exceed your expectations of yourselves and others. Passion is its own perpetual-motion fuel.

"Nurturing awareness of the importance of the purpose is a key to keeping passion intense and impactful in an organization. It is critical to find and engage people who can subscribe to and become passionate about the organization's purpose—why it exists—is an important dimension in the daily functioning of the business."

"I agree with that and feel we've done a good job of making our purpose clear to all of our stakeholders. It has an impact on everyone our company touches," says Diane.

* * *

Clear and Succinct

* * *

Cal continues, "Defining the purpose in clear and succinct terms is a start. For some, it may be one or two words and, for others, a full statement. It most often carries the message of what is done for others or for a purpose that is larger than the individuals in the organization. Building lives and stories around it helps it grow and become the outsized reason people in the organization are continually motivated. The online tools provide a place to post the purpose and another place for others to share relevant and illustrative stories. They share firsthand and secondhand experiences that occur within the company.

"This makes them a part of the story and lore of the company. It becomes a journal of the journey, with a focus on how everyone is doing something important together that makes good things happen for lots of other people. It is in the doing, and not just in the talking about it, that the impact is amplified.

$$* * *$$

Do it for the benefit of others

$$* * *$$

Diane says, "We don't capture our stories, but they are occurring. When they happen, we talk about them, but then it dies down and…they're not lost, just tucked way too far in the background. I like this idea of the journal and having everyone share their experiences. Is there more to this?"

Cal replies, "With the online tools, the stories are placed in the journal. There are also features that allow others in the company to make comments about each story. This allows each incident to become its own longer story, with tentacles that reach deep into the company. Many of these stories won't necessarily end up on a company's website or in its brochure, but they are important to the people involved. Keeping them inside sometimes adds greater value. So we're talking about the stories that would otherwise get ignored or mentioned only in passing. Giving them more airtime adds significant value. This becomes an opportunity for all team members to have enlarged views and opinions about how important their roles are in the company. This is very good."

Diane says, "I think this may be one of the most important impacts of fully and deliberately implementing the big parts. Is there anything else?"

"Yes, there are other things like the organization's mission and vision, but, for now, we'll hold off on those. We'll develop those along the journey. They also add value to this important big part."

* * *

Let your heart race

* * *

"And one important thing is that it's all about what is in your heart and everyone's around you. Do it all so that it impacts your and others' hearts. That doesn't mean you can't do it with discipline. It doesn't mean you can't do it efficiently and effectively and in full support of numbers. I just caution that it is important to let the heart rule, and the numbers will follow and serve the heart well.

"I'd like to emphasize one last point while we're on this topic. A primary reason for developing and pressing the importance of purpose is to inspire all those on your team as well as other stakeholders. It is also necessary to emphasize that chaos in an organization reduces the impact of inspiration. It's essential to facilitate a leading and managing framework to bring order and focus to the inspired ones."

Summary

It's essential to establish right things for the whole of the company and the functional parts. Getting them done in the right way is even more important. Stopping to define and refine the right things should be a scheduled and deliberate priority. Doing this correctly is where working smart happens so working hard can create real value.

Why an organization exists and what it accomplishes are the most important contributing factors in generating passion. Passion is the perpetual fuel that causes great organizations to flourish and soar in exceptional ways. People want to be part of something that transcends their personal focus and helps them know they are doing good things for the benefit of others. They want to touch their hearts and the hearts of others. This is a mark of civilized people.

Inspiration is essential. We must also provide an ordered environment in which the inspired ones can work together effectively.

Customer Service
shouldn't be
a department;
it should be
the entire company.

—*Tony Hsieh, CEO of zappos.com*

8. BIG PART 2: CUSTOMERS

Choose and serve customers passionately

Cal asks, "Is your organization customer focused?"

"Yes, we absolutely are! Everything we do is assessed by how it will impact the customer."

Cal persists. "If I were to ask others in your organization whether the company is customer focused, I expect they would say yes as well. Here is my question around this. Are they customer focused in the same way you are? Are all of you on the same page about it?"

Diane responds, "I'm not sure we're all on the exact same page about it, but I'd bet we're close. It's a part of all of our conversations and our activities. We never lose sight of the customer."

"That's a very good answer. I'm proposing a bit of a refinement, because as you grow, you'll need to have the new people on the same page. They must share your heart and mind about what it means to be customer focused. Is that a reasonable thought?"

Diane answers, "Of course. It is certainly our expectation."

Cal asks, "Do you have a document that you could hand me that would convince me beyond a shadow of doubt that you and the others are actively and consistently in full agreement about how your company lives its customer-focused commitment?"

"I'm not sure what you mean by a document."

Cal continues, "I'm talking about a document that describes your customer focus philosophy, principles, activities, descriptions, measurements, and body of teaching you do toward it throughout the company. You are like the best companies in that you talk about it all the time. I'm hoping to convince you that refinement is possible that will transform this important big part in your business. Are you open to listen to this a bit more?"

"Yes," responds Diane. "You have me curious with a sense that we're getting into a bit of Eastern-style thinking and exchange where you ask questions for which I can't possibly have your desired answers."

"To a certain extent that is true. My motive is to gauge your sensitivity to this issue and, at the same time, suggest there is an opportunity for improvement. My understanding from your assessment is that you're doing well already. I'm also thinking you are more customer focused in the sales and marketing parts and less so in the operational parts of the company.

"One thought for you to ponder as we progress is how much of the time spent is being reactive to customer issues and how much time is spent being proactive. However, you will find that with what I'm proposing, we can get this to a new standard for you. Also it will put in place a set of tools and processes that will allow you to grow rapidly and still keep everyone on the same page.

"You will have a one-page document that outlines your customer focus to attract, engage, serve, and nurture customers. Everyone who will give you two to three minutes to explain it will easily understand it."

"OK, I'm open to that and am now feeling less defensive."

Cal continues, "It should all start with the customer. Build the organization from the customer experience. If the company is already underway, let's go back and build it again, but without changing anything until the design is done. To do that, you have to capture and understand it all from the customer perspective. It's not just about the products/services. It's who the organization is and how it does its things.

"It's taking the character of the organization and structuring around it so that everyone in the organization understands customer focus and uses it to do their daily activities. This is necessary for operational excellence and the ongoing ability to innovate at the same time. There's a quote attributed to Steve Jobs that I like. 'You've got to start with the customer experience and work back toward the technology—not the other way around.'

"This doesn't apply only to creating technology products/services but for creating and selling any product or service. It is important that an organization be able to say, '*We build our company around the customer experience every day.*' The usual alternative, although never overtly talked about, is, 'We manipulate what we do each day to serve our customers so that they will like what we do.' To do this in the correct way—build around the customer—there must be a discipline of seeing it, doing it, documenting it, and helping everyone understand it simply and clearly every day. This allows all employees to operate effectively and efficiently and be able to add their special twists to each touch with clients."

Diane asks, "How do you do that?"

"At the Zynity Leadership™ website, there is a tool or app designated as the C-Vyoos™. It is the acronym for the <u>C</u>ustomer <u>v</u>iew of <u>y</u>our <u>o</u>rganization's <u>o</u>peration<u>s</u>. It's a template that guides teams to input their current operating content into a format that helps them picture how the customers see their operations. It takes about an hour to get the basics in place in the template. Then the team can work together for another couple of hours and expand their understanding. This is a place where the organizing-the-garage concept is really in play."

* * *

Customer view of your organization's operations

* * *

"There are a whole bunch of things going on in various parts of the organization. But how they fit and work together is not always developed and presented in an easily understood whole. This template makes that possible. The principles of 'headline speak' are fully in play here as the tool/app forces the team to use key words and short phrases to describe the many parts.

"A puzzle analogy works here. This app puts all the current information into a form that establishes the borders first. This makes locating where the inside pieces fit more easily understood. The key understanding is how the pieces or the functional parts work together— or should work together. Once the first draft of content is in this template, it becomes clear how the team can use it to expand how they work together better.

"It becomes a great sales tool and also the one-page table of contents for the digital operations manual. The design maximizes both the sales and the operational parts of being customer focused. Each of the sound bites in the boxes, together with the steps in the matrix form, becomes a section of the operations manual. A double click on a box expands it into a table of contents for the individual box and all of the relevant forms and documents needed for the operations in that box.

* * *

Digital operations manual

* * *

"With this working, it provides a digitally accessible operations manual—that few companies have—designed around how the company attracts, engages, serves, and nurtures customers. Each person in the company has access to it at all times, and the updates are immediately available when posted by authorized parties.

Diane says, "I'm having a hard time picturing this. It seems confusing and complicated."

"Let me show you a diagram or matrix that is the process by which a company attracts, engages, and supports its customers."

Cal shows Diane a one-page document with ten columns and six rows. The rows are distinct and separate. The first row establishes the titles for each of the columns, and the columns are connected in each of the rows. The rows are labeled (1) Stages, (2) Results, (3) Activities, (4) Contributors, (5) Helpers, and (6) Reports.

"The matrix describes the features of the experience from the customer's perspective in simple and concise headlines."

* * *

Must get it all on one page

* * *

After reading through the matrix on the following page, Diane comments, "So this goes beyond just the sales cycle. It includes how the organization extends its relationships with customers. And, in the lower rows, it summarizes for each stage of the customer relationship the items necessary for operations to do their parts. It's complicated, but simple. It states the highlights in a few words for each box in the matrix. This is the start?"

Zynity's Process to Attract, Engage, and Support Organizations

™C-Vyoos - The "Customer's View" of Zynity, LLC's Organization and Operations

Stages	Become Aware	Connect	Share	Committed Organization	Schedule	Training	Support	Follow-up Training	Support	Ongoing Success
Results	Focus Credibility Relationships Attract	Understanding	Show Tools Educate Select	Clear Documented Agreement Sign-up	Confirm Start Date	Motivate & Train Administrator	Phone & Chat Support Certified Partner	Equip Individual Growth	All Orgs Engaged Properly	Continued & Expanded Participation by Users
Activities	P R Personal Calls Networking Conferences City Launch	Research Discussions Meetings Presentations	Show Tools & Value to Organizations	Clarification Agreement Signing	Specify All Resources & Required Dates	Online or Face-Face Meetings	Proactive & Reactive Communication	Online or Face-Face Meetings	Proactive & Reactive Communication	Monitor Analyze Report Adjust
Contributors	Strategy Sales Marketing	Sales Tele-Sales Certified Partner	Sales CPs	Sales CPs	Training Team Support Staff	Trainers Certified Partner	Trainers Support Staff Certified Partner	Trainers CPs	Trainers CPs Support Staff	Communications Marketing CPs
Helpers	Books Website City Launch Webinars Seminars	Assessment Information Research Analysis Value	Agenda Process Web Tools Samples Website Demo	Product Quality Value Add & Reputation	Website Support Staff	Processes Website Books Tutorials	Qualified Trainers Website Tutorials	Processes Website Exercises Testing	Support Staff Trainers Website	Website New Dimensions Community Communication
Reports	# of Org Leads # New Contacts # Attracted	# of Requests for Next Step	# of Requests for Training # Selected	# of Sign-ups # Orgs in Pipeline	# of Confirmed Dates # in Schedule	# of Orgs # of Users in Training	# of Incident Reports & Status	# of Orgs # of Tools Next Migration	# of Incident Reports	# Active Orgs # Tables/Org # Users/Table # Tools/Table # of Referrals

Cal responds, "Yes, this is the start. Each of the boxes will have more information within them once they are accessed. All this fits within the earlier discussions around headlines and concise statements. It also becomes a central place for each part to know more about what the other parts are doing. Each can read the others' boxes of information and discuss them with one another to make learning easier. Also it becomes the place where we standardize terminology so we all get better at speaking the same language."

Diane says, "I understand enough of this for now. It will take a bit of work. It can be done in short bursts of time to get it started. A discipline of adding our changes will happen as we make them on an ongoing basis."

* * *

Proof of customer focus

* * *

Cal adds, "Then you will have a document that proves you're customer focused. Your customer focus is deliberately designed around the full life cycle of your customer and done in a one-page format that expands into a fully digital operations manual."

"I like that," says Diane. "This makes some sense to me now. I can see that with a little work, my team and I can develop this very well."

Cal continues, "If you are passionate about the needs of the customers you are working so hard to attract, then it will make each day a lovefest. If the others on your team share this passion and know you are genuine, then they will enjoy the entire process as well. By having this type of tool active, all will know that you are organized, engaged, and ready for the next stages of growth."

Summary

Being customer focused is essential. Often it is more talked about than organized and implemented. Methodologies and digital tools can help make it easier to be customer focused as well as more uniformly understood throughout a company. Making the complex simple sometimes requires attention to details in a process that demands being concise and results in a summary that carries a much bigger message.

*Coming together
is a beginning;
Keeping together
is progress;
Working together
is success.*

—Henry Ford

9. BIG PART 3: MANAGING TEAM

Step one for implementing greatness

Cal continues, "Getting the managing team working together is significantly different from getting them to work individually. Getting the functional parts working together in a manner that qualifies as more than collegial collaboration is not easily attained. Getting them connected with top-level communicating capabilities, having them share passionately about the same purpose, and then melding them together with a common culture is foundational for getting them to work together.

"Signs that they work together is that each knows at all times the top priorities of the organization as well as the top priorities needed for each one on the team to lead and manage their functional part of the organization. They should each know how their parts work in conjunction with the other parts, as well as how their parts work within their own walls. The people in their functional teams must also understand the hows and whys and whats of the other functional teams and always be eager to engage in helping them exceed their goals and overcome their current obstacles. This marks a team with distinction. If not, it's like a bicycle with a broken or missing part; it will not work."

* * *

Each must know the others' parts

* * *

"How do you get people to do that when they all have more than enough to do in their own areas?" asks Diane.

"I'm very glad you asked how. I take that to mean that you see some value in having this happen if there's a way to do it."

Diane replies, "Yes, I do. I'm eager to see how we do it and how we teach others it really helps."

"First we get the team fully passionate about purpose. Then we make sure we are living within the premises of our culture every day. We must know one another's headlines and priorities and embrace that it is our portion to care about everyone else's areas. We will possess all the ingredients required to make everyone live as if they are the keeper of the others' worlds. They don't have to do the work of the other parts. They just have to be aware of them and know how they get done. In a broad sense, this is how you, as the principal leader, feel. It will be good if the whole team can have the same perspective and sense of caring about the others as you have."

"I'm not sure I get all that. Do you mean that all we need is to be aware of and care about what the other parts are doing?" asks Diane.

Cal replies, "It may not seem like much, but is it being deliberately accomplished in your company today?"

"Well, I think it happens to some extent quite a bit of the time."

Cal replies, "I agree that it's like that to some extent. What I'm suggesting is for it to be done all the time and deliberately. Then it will be done in a way that is impactful and not just ad hoc or because two of your leaders happen to get along. This must become a defined big part that is woven through the whole company, is practiced as a matter of course, and people get better at it each day."

"OK, so what you're pressing here is that it has to be done overtly, and we need to expect it as a matter of course," says Diane.

* * *

Do what you do better

* * *

Cal responds, "Yes. Most of the things I want you to do more deliberately already occur to some extent in your organization. We want to continue doing them but with better results. A key value of the framework is to establish new standards of performance. New standards occur only if all the organization's big parts are used fully and deliberately every day. There must also be ongoing initiatives to make each functional part better. Remember earlier when I used the analogy of cleaning up the garage?"

* * *

Organize and increase discipline

* * *

Cal continues, "This is an example of that. You have many very good things going on and being done in this organization. The system and the online tools will help you get them organized, establish a better discipline of using them, and create an environment where all the people know about the system and how their parts and the others fit within the system. These big parts and the online tools make that possible. It will never be perfect, but it will be better than how it's happening now, which is haphazardly."

* * *

Haphazard is not a virtue

* * *

"So you think we're doing many things right, and you haven't even been to the company yet? Are you just saying that so I won't be offended and refuse to start your journey?" asks Diane.

Cal replies, "So you think I'm trying to manipulate you into starting this journey by being both good cop and bad cop?"

Diane responds, "I certainly think that's possible."

"It certainly is," replies Cal. "But let me attempt to explain in another way what I mean by all this. I don't need to go to your company to see what is being done because I have been to so many that I already know the general conditions that apply to what we're doing here. I know the symptoms. I know you are responding to symptoms and not the problems. You are open to learning, and, at this point, you think I may be giving you a one-size-fits-all form of consulting platitudes.

"That is not the case. Your problem is that you have no system for leading and managing, and you're not able to organize and lead your team as well as you'd like. It takes way more effort and time on your part than you ever imagined. And this situation makes you feel the limitations of doing it how you're doing it.

"Harken back to our earlier exchange around golf and the index. I told you then that you don't have to give up all that you're presently doing. You just have to take on a few new things to get even more out of what you're already doing. Does this sound similar to and consistent with what I shared a few minutes ago that made you defensive and annoyed?"

"Yes."

"I also said we would use the concepts and online tools to get your content into a more organized and useful condition. I'm introducing you to a different way of thinking about what you do. The addition of a framework can make everything more measurable and repeatable and teachable to a broader audience in a consistent manner.

"It makes all of the employees active in the system, and this helps them learn faster. This helps you become a true learning and teaching organization with many more active learners and teachers.

"You will no longer bring new people in and just send them off to 'do their things' without them understanding how people who are running another functional part 'do their things.' Other people need to teach them how they do their 'things.' It needs to be collegial and collaborative rather than just competitive. They need to have a shared goal rather than a sense of competing for scarce resources so that they can do better than the other parts."

Diane asks, "Why say 'just' competitive? Shouldn't there be competitiveness?"

* * *

Being competitive correctly is good

* * *

"Yes, it's important for people to be competitive even within the team. Each one should work to the best at doing all the company stands for. Everyone should want to be the best at what they, do and their intensity of effort should be points of competitiveness. We don't want them to compete in doing something to slow down or thwart another part in such a way it will diminish the performance of the organization as a whole. For this, they need to share common goals and be committed and understanding of one another's points of success.

"The principal leader must put these things in place, and then encourage the team by teaching them to teach everyone else. This creates a real team, in which members incite one another to their own definition of standards of excellence. This requires a system that is simple and elegant that everyone understands and has bought into. Out of this behavior and the reinforcement of the right behaviors and attitudes, a culture develops in the company."

Cultures aren't so much planned
as they evolve
from that early set of people.

—*Jeff Bezos, CEO of Amazon*

* * *

Culture must be designed as it evolves

* * *

Cal continues, "Culture is one of the most important dimensions of the Managing Team big part in an organization. It sets the hearts and minds of the entire team to think about, do, say, and relate to all parts of the organization. In most companies, it develops over time based on the personalities, incidents, industry, and successes or failures. It's important to engage in a more deliberate process of establishing, defining, and nurturing your organization's culture. What are your thoughts Diane?"

"I know we have one, and, at this point, it seems to be helping us. We paid attention to defining our values, and we work hard to do our business activities within the bounds of our value system. I also believe values both shape and reflect one's sense of responsibility. We think there may be more needed for this as we grow, but for now we're happy with where we are and what we're doing along these lines. Do you have additional thoughts?"

Cal responds, "I agree with you and all companies have a culture they just may not have developed it deliberately. Usually culture just evolves without much attention. Considering what you've said, you're likely well ahead of where most companies are with this, and I would like to talk about it with you for a few minutes. We'll do much more once we're engaged in implementing the whole system in your company. I'm just reminding both of us that today we're addressing what this is and why you should do it.

"I think the ingredients of a culture encompass values, principles, attitudes, habits, traditions, styles, behaviors, and experiences of the key influencers. It determines how the organization sets priorities, chooses strategies, selects people, and sets expectations.

"Culture is equal to the sum of its ingredients and the emphasis or coefficients or weight put on each ingredient. If an organization says it includes an ingredient in its list but doesn't include it in its practice, that isn't good. There needs to be a way to identify what is being used and what is being ignored. In an algebraic formula expression it would look like this."

Cal scribbles the following formula on a napkin: Culture = I1 + I2 + I3 +I4.

"*I* is the character used to designate the name of each ingredient," Cal says. "Also note that they are additive one with the other.

"It can also be modified and more fully understood if we establish the relative importance of each ingredient by adding a coefficient so the equation would look like this."

Cal writes another formula below the first one. This one reads, "Culture = .5I1 + .7I2 + .4I3 + .2I4."

"I know this seems a bit tedious at first. In a couple of one-hour exercises with you and your team, we can put your ingredients into an equation that you'll like and understand. There is a need to give its definition some priority. It allows you to picture what you're really made of and the relative importance of each ingredient. To start with I would not worry about trying to assign coefficients, but that will come as you get better at understanding and discussing your culture.

"It's important to discuss specific incidents on an ongoing basis and assess how the actions and words involved fit or move within the culture. As you no doubt expect, the learning and adjusting never stops. The attention frequency and passion about it evolves, and accelerates or diminishes its intended impact. It's never fixed, and, yet, it's always setting the desired standards."

Diane asks, "What do you mean it's never fixed? Should we adhere to our values and principles with little or no wavering? Isn't that what they are, anchors or absolutes?"

* * *

Cultures evolve

* * *

"They aren't absolutes, but they should be anchors that connect us to a foundation. They are more like a foundation that puts a standard in place, and then we all work from there. They become less absolute when we add the dynamics of our behaviors and styles. Let's use the example of being open and honest as a culture ingredient. Some people think that in order to be open and honest about confronting a mistake it can only be shared properly if it's done boldly, emphatically, and bluntly. Another may feel it can be done gently and at the right time with the right preparation. For example, I may assess something to be a mistake, and yet, I may not confront the person immediately upon discovery (be open) because it would derail that person for the moment. Some people like to confront by saying don't do that and others like to confront by saying this is what you should do. Keeping that person on course for the moment may be more important than sharing a harsh and strongly worded assessment.

"I may follow through with being open and honest later when that person is in a better situation to receive it, learn from it, and become better for it. Also, it brings up the thoughts around the different meanings and intonations around the words, blunt, bold, callous, and so forth. Culture covers both substance and style. Does that make sense?"

Diane replies, "Yes, it does, but it adds more confusion and complexity that I'm not ready to take on right now."

Cal pauses before responding. "I understand how you feel. We can make implementation complex or simple. This is how we make it simple. You do a bit of research and develop a list of the values from *The Book of Virtues*, written by William J. Bennett. This becomes the base list, and, from there, we add items gathered from looking at the culture, value, or mission statements of other companies' websites. Then we'll have a meeting with your team to discuss them, and out of that will come an accepted list and a sentence of definition that applies to your organization for each item in the list."

Diane says, "I know this is necessary. Why can't we just have a couple of us develop a list and put it on our website?"

Cal responds, "Engaging others in the development process is necessary. It creates a part of the culture that says our deliberate attention to establishing culture is important to all of us. As a coaching point, I believe a major milestone for you will be when you are as intense and focused on building others as you are with improving yourself.

"Their commitment will blossom and their adherence to the culture will come naturally as a matter of course. Then we'll add an additional step using the online tools. There is a place for them to post each incident that illustrates how they, or someone else, did something that exemplified adherence to the culture."

* * *

Culture must engage everyone

* * *

"The folklore of the company will begin with and flourish with this. The listing of accumulated incidents will tell a story of the heart and mind of the company. In the tools, individuals can add their comments, questions, and accolades about each incident so the celebration part will remain as well. The foundation of the company is its all-encompassing heart and mind as expressed in the dynamics of its values, principles, behaviors, and styles. You and the others in the leading and managing team will morph the culture by how you add your comments to the incidents as they are reported."

Diane says, "I want an imbedded part of our culture and practices to include intensity about a gradual and steady improvement in all the things we do. Ongoing personal, professional, and organizational improvement must be one of the marks of our culture."

"Your statement is spectacular. Think! In most companies, the people are not aware of the culture items. In your company, they will learn to see them in action, and then be excited to celebrate them. This will establish the dynamic of your culture. Over time, it will be further imbedded into all parts of the company. The behaviors and styles will adjust how the culture is applied in the activities of the company."

"How do you keep everyone working within the culture if it seems so complex?" asks Diane.

* * *

Cultures must morph

* * *

"The complexity you think about with the list of ingredients and the coefficients surfaces only occasionally when changes are made to it. It's in the recording of the incidents and sharing in simple ways where the value is created. It's simple for people to do that with a small amount of training. They just share a story and identify which ingredient or ingredients are amplified in it. They'll learn to keep it simple. The strength of the foundation is that it's made to be prominent and dynamic. It becomes more than just a list on a website or a statement in an employee manual or part of the strategic planning three-ring binder on a shelf. It's alive and active daily within all employees."

Summary

The dynamics created by an engaging leading and managing system that pulls all the parts together and gets them working together is essential for excellence. It requires definition, discipline, and commitment.

Getting the management team interactive and interdependent is a major accomplishment. Understanding in some depth what each member on the team does helps the team come together in new ways.

A well-formed, implemented, and morphing culture is one of an organization's greatest strengths. It starts simple and stays simple with use. It's in the use that its impact is maximized. It creates value in all parts of the organization.

What's measured improves.

—*Peter F. Drucker*

10. BIG PART 4: MEASUREMENTS

Measure to gauge and celebrate

"Diane, what are the most important measurements or reports for your organization?"

Diane quickly replies, "The ones that come to mind first are sales, cash flow, and profits. These are the ones I'm most concerned about for the overall health of the company."

Cal responds, "Great answers. These come from the gauges for the top level of your organization. Without solid sales, cash flow, and profits, a company is in trouble. These three measurements aggregate the efforts and results of many areas in the company. It is imperative that you know your numbers and in the right time frame.

"You asked about nonprofits in our first phone call, and this may be the right time to address them. I think you said you're on a nonprofit board and want to be helpful with how it is managed."

Diane replies, "That's right. I have enjoyed being a part of it and learning to see the world from their eyes and heart."

Cal continues, "Nonprofits are also concerned about contributions and balances. However, there is a big leap from the sources of their contributions to the services they provide. The receivers of their services are usually not the ones who provide the contributions. In your company, those getting the services provide the contributions.

"I want to linger on this just long enough to point out the difference in profit versus nonprofit, and then we'll make the point later that the operating measurements will be similar. Yes, running a for-profit organization is different from running a nonprofit, but there are also many similarities."

$$* * *$$

Nonprofits and for-profits

$$* * *$$

Diane says, "I can see that running an organization of either type would have many similarities. There just seems to be a bit of contention generally that nonprofits have more heart, and for-profits have no heart. They just want to make a profit no matter what. I don't believe it's any easier to manage people and resources in a nonprofit environment. I also know it's not easy to manage to tight budgets in a non-profit. Without profit or margin, any organization will quickly close, unless an investment provides cash. Leading and managing both require lots of heart for all stakeholders.

"However, investment in any organization is done with the expectation of careful management of people and resources. All organizations require leading and man-aging to sustain and grow. I make these points to let you know that I respect and appreciate those who lead and manage nonprofits as much as I do those who lead and manage for-profits."

Cal says, "I agree with you and feel that both need to be engaged with what they measure and manage to assure their present and future."

"So the basic economic concept of leading and man-aging in an environment of scarce and/or restricted resources is applicable to both types of entities," adds Diane.

"I agree, and I'm glad we took that rabbit trail. I want to use it to move to a discussion about mea-suring and managing the daily, weekly, and monthly items that are at the mid and operational levels. I don't want to spend time itemizing all the various kinds of reports but rather establish some principles and practices that guide the development and use of these reports.

* * *

Centralized list of reports

* * *

"Do you maintain a central list of all the reports and the key measurements in those reports for each area of the organization?"

Before she can respond Cal also asks, "How often do you review reporting with the teams? I'm thinking about such things as who gets the reports and what you expect them to do or make happen with the contents of the reporting."

Diane responds, "We have selected reports that we meet around and discuss. Some we look at daily, some weekly, and some monthly. We have a number of reports, and people use them."

Cal responds, "I'm sure that is true, but in this measurements big part, we're looking for an added dimension. It's important that you build a list of all the reports used in each functional area. We want this list to contain a title, area, purpose, owner, creator, recipients, and the expectations we have for each recipient. There can be other items, but I'm sure you see we're looking for the framework of the report and reporting so it can be assessed and reviewed on a scheduled basis.

"I visualize a quarterly meeting for each area in which all of their reports are reviewed with the deliberate purposes of giving light to things that are presently in the dark, identifying opportunities for letting everyone know, and acknowledging that you care about all they are doing. Even though you don't engage with it daily, you do engage with it regularly, and you support the importance of every detail. This establishes you as the leader of reporting veracity and quality. It also sends a clear message that you understand and acknowledge the spectacular importance of the details. By sharing this in meetings, it becomes a public display of your respect for them and their importance."

* * *

All must respect the details

* * *

"For contrast, consider that in the early days, you were probably aware of all these details. Now others contend with them. The important thing you do with this quarterly meeting is ask questions. One, are these the right things to measure. Two, do they help us. Three, who are the ones using them correctly. The issue is not just the detail of the reports but the framework, structure, and discipline around both creating and using the reports. This will differentiate you from every other organization that your employees have worked in. In this process, you demonstrate both your understanding that the details are critical and your organizational skills that keep you and everyone else engaged at both a detail and conceptual level.

"An example is a helpful event in which the creator of a report stops distribution, and then waits to see who calls to ask for the report and how quickly. This helps identify reporting that should be changed or people who should be trained to start using reports they are presently ignoring. It's not about you determining all the reports that are needed. Rather, it's about working with your team to establish a set of principles and practices that reinforce your sense of value around the importance of measuring so that the details can be managed.

* * *

Reporting must be disciplined

* * *

"Reporting is expensive. It needs guidelines and an associated discipline of assessment and review that includes all those that are connected with them. This helps them ask better "why" questions and helps them make sure they are paying proper attention to all the details. Does that make sense to you?"

Diane replies, "Yes, it makes perfect sense. It's about engaging them in the process of reviewing and assessing the what, why, and how of our reporting. This also gives me and the other leaders an opportunity to build and share our principles and philosophies about how a particular part of the business should be measured. It also establishes a proactive attention to these things so we aren't just reacting after a failure."

Cal responds, "I agree. You do understand the basics of all this. We will discuss more about this later, but, for now, you get the major points very well. I would like to add these couple of thoughts.

"Reporting and highlighting by exception is a common principle. This makes it easier to spot issues and take actions about issues before they become bigger problems."

* * *

Measure for recognition

* * *

"Measurements are for more than just holding others accountable. They also determine how well someone is doing in order to recognize their successes. They help establish standards that can be adhered to and goals that can be surpassed. Numbers are important. How one uses numbers must be even more important.

"In a sense, an organization is like a big and complex puzzle. It's different in that everything changes and moves all the time. Measurements are the border pieces. They help establish a border and help it keep its shape. Get them in place and pay attention to them, and the rest of the puzzle will be more manageable. This concept is true for the big picture, and its essence applies for the individual pieces."

Summary

A common error in small and midsize business is the absence of consistent attention to the measurement of the right things. Measuring so that you can manage implies control over others. It can also be used to reduce the need for control over people and allow them to participate in setting their own measures and take more control over their own lives. Measurements establish the framework and boundaries that are necessary for managing the daily activities as well identifying the next most important areas for ongoing improvement.

Harmony can be achieved
when each unique person
deliberately commits
and works to fit
well with all others
in their organization.

—*Dwaine Canova*

11. HARMONY

Harmony uses tension and difference for good

Cal continues, "While implementing the big parts, it's important to begin thinking about an important concept that must accompany this new thinking and these new behaviors. You can assess whether it gets established properly by knowing we are getting all the parts to play well together. It's an ongoing mix of leading and managing at the same time.

"The tools provide discipline and guidance to bring order to strategies, values, and culture to better attract and serve customers. They also add attention to the items that must be measured to manage all the moving parts of an organization. This helps define and continually refine the leading and managing of the top level, as well as the other levels.

"I like to begin with 'understanding' and 'seeing' what disciplined leading and managing should accomplish for an organization with the word 'harmony.' Harmony creates happiness and humor. It takes different voices and makes them sound better together than they would alone. Harmony creates a feeling, along with leverage and synergy in organizations, with a single effort. It takes different individuals and makes them play better together than they would alone. Musical groups are an example. Team sports are another, and so is a crew on a ship.

* * *

Concinnity

* * *

"I want to introduce a new word for the sake of adding an important dimension to the understanding of an important dynamic about teams. The word is 'concinnity,' which means the skillful and harmonious arrangement or fitting together of the different parts of something. I'm excited about this unique word because it's about putting things together and includes the word 'harmony.' The new dynamic is needed to add to the meanings of synergy (creation of more than the sum of the parts) and leverage (extending to exert more force). The words 'synergy' and 'leverage' are used often but they don't include the feelings that accompany the word 'harmony.'"

* * *

Good tension need not create contention

* * *

"Making this 'better together' phenomenon more prevalent in organizations should be one of our signature passions. It requires structure, discipline, and deliberate attention to good feelings to make moments of needed tension opportunities for growth and not the beginnings of unnecessary or negative contention.

"Harmony is created with the simultaneous use of distinctly different elements. It is not about eliminating conflict but, rather, orchestrating the parts to get the desired results. Because the elements are different, there is deliberate tension. The togetherness of the opposing tension of the elements creates the quality of the harmony…element one and element two and element three and element four and so on…The larger the number of elements, the greater the marvel when harmony is created. Each element needs to be more aware of how it fits within the whole than it does about how it exists on its own. No part in an organization should think it can exist alone. It needs to always do its part to its extreme best, but it is never alone. An organization is like a mobile. If one part moves, so will the others."

* * *

"And"

* * *

"Leaders and managers working together make their organizations great…great to work in and great in performance. It's about the 'and.' It's rare for a great organization to exist for a length of time in which great to work in or great in performance is missing. I have not observed such a company. Leaders and managers who create harmony generate great performance from the people in the organization."

* * *

Leaders must manage and managers must lead

* * *

"An important premise is that leaders must also manage and managers must also lead. In many cases, they must do both at the same time. While doing something in the 'present,' it is important to consider how it has meaning and impact for other parts and the 'future.' While considering and contending with 'outside' issues, it is essential to be concerned about how they impact 'inside.' Leadership is future and externally focused. Management is present and internally focused. The definitions and many of the required skill sets are essentially polar opposites. In small and midsize businesses, the principal leader and the management team must be capable of doing both simultaneously with a high degree of skill."

* * *

Harmony requires deliberate effort

* * *

"Harmony does not happen easily. It is best established with a deep and broad understanding of the separate elements. An appreciation for how these elements work together increases the value and result of their combination. Individuals who appreciate and understand one another can create and experience harmony. Leaders and managers make this either possible or impossible. They must also instill and amplify the individual excitement and passions to seek harmony."

* * *

Hearts and minds, emotions and intellect

* * *

"These are matters of the heart as well as the mind. One without the other will be significantly less. It is not just about facts and figures or goals and objectives. It is also about feelings and emotions. Oops! I hope that statement doesn't offend you. Elaborate attention to measurements does not eliminate the need for awareness of feelings. Nor, does elaborate attention to feelings eliminate the need for measurements. This tension, lead and managed properly, creates greatness.

"Organizations have many elements and elements within elements. They are complex and multidimensional. Establishing a framework with boundaries and rules is difficult, but essential. The framework should be static, with opportunities for flexibility as change occurs. How the elements work together within the framework comprises the dynamics that determine its power to create and produce.

"Running an organization of any type or size day to day is incredibly complex and multidimensional. Without clarity of how the big parts weave through the entire organization, the functional parts will operate without a deliberate sense of belonging together."

$$* * *$$

Elements maintain their individuality

$$* * *$$

"Elements get connected with other elements without losing their individuality. Together, they are better than they are separately. Being trained in a system that teaches one to recognize harmony makes one more capable of participating in it."

Summary

Harmony creates a better foundation when using leverage to create synergy. Harmony is not the glue that holds the parts together but the catalyst and/or mystical ingredient that amplifies the interactions of distinctly different parts to get desired results. Working together better is a worthy ongoing effort and objective.

*I've learned that people
will forget
what you said,
people will forget
what you did,
but people will
never forget
how you
made them feel.*

— *Maya Angelou, American author, poet, dancer,
actress, and singer*

12. PEOPLE

They are everywhere

Cal continues, "No matter where you turn in leading and managing an enterprise, there they are—people! They are the source of joy and the frustration of it all ('and' again!). They are wonderful and horrible. Their great diversity is a marvel as individuals and within their individuality. Organizations that deliberately work to help people exceed their own expectations will transform the people, the organization, and all parts of the world they touch. I mention this as I have heard leaders comment more than once about how their businesses would be better and simpler were it not for customers and employees."

Diane says, "I've never said it, but I have heard others say it. I may have thought it a time or two."

Cal says, "People would be (and would desire to be) wonderful all the time in all circumstances were it not for their individual human natures. We can explain each individual's negative aberrations as being unable to separate from their own humanity. This diversity is simply not their fault and, in fact, is their great strength. So we must remind ourselves of that fact as we humbly work through the difficulties of nurturing customers, employees, vendors, governments, and all the other people. These 'people' comprise the bulk of the uncontrollable moving parts that dart in and out of the lives of those in leadership and management roles.

"They cannot be moved aside, nor can their complexity be eliminated even partially. I accept them and respect them, and I find them exasperating in certain circumstances. This tension between respect and exasperation highlights the need to establish an organization that accepts everyone at all times, no matter the circumstances. Circumstances pass. Yes, it may be appropriate to help one move to another organization, but it should be done with respect and consideration."

$$* * *$$

Employees are people

$$* * *$$

"Great employees are nurtured from ordinary people. The organization's culture and the leadership and management techniques can help wonderful people display their greatness. Also, poor leadership and management can help wonderful people become disengaged and perform far below their potentials."

Diane says, "I have a deep desire for the employees in our organization to know they are respected and appreciated at all times. I also want them to be the kind of people who push their own envelopes to continue growing as people and to help our organization grow."

"That is paramount," says Cal. "The tools help build the connections and engagement with the leading and managing process so the people understand the system and can operate it and operate within it. All they do is more visible to others on the team. Each individual has more input and impacts within the system and in the way things are supposed to be done within the company.

"All people at all levels need to be engaged to some extent with the implementation of the system. And because there is a system that is defined and tangible, it is more real and easier for everyone to relate to. I say that because every organization has a system, even if they don't work at defining and clarifying it. It just may not be clear or deliberately shared so that everyone can know how it really works."

Diane says, "I've been thinking about this as we've talked today. We already have a system, but it's not defined and shared in a deliberate way with everyone. Many parts of what we already do will fit very well within the new system. That encourages me."

"I'm sure you're correct," says Cal. "In a while, we'll start exploring the use of the online tools, but, before we do that, I want to get a sense of your buy-in to this adventure. What are your feelings at the moment?"

Diane replies, "I'm feeling inclined to do this. I'm trying to determine if I know enough to explain to my team why. In fact, I'm thinking we should probably present it to our management team as a possibility and see if we can get their buy-in, so it will be their decision as well."

Cal says, "I agree with you completely. I would, however, like for you and I to construct a presentation and session with them that includes you expressing a credible understanding of all this and how it fits within your style. We want them to accurately perceive this as an initiative and journey that will benefit everyone individually as well as the company.

"The view we must share is of an organization that takes into account the desire for learning and capabilities of everyone in the organization. The methodology helps put in place an environment of innovation and change that is not completely dependent upon one person or a select few."

Cal continues, "It must bring into play all the talent in the organization. A framework will be established in which there is structure and order. Individuals will input their strengths on a continuous basis and get recognized for their contributions."

* * *

All the talent is needed

* * *

"These new concepts and new tools will help you get to the new place where you need to be and want to be. You will build a new culture and environment in which others can flourish. It is a win-win-win for everyone.

"If we sincerely believe the view is worth the climb, we will get there faster. It needs to be, for everyone, all about the people. Numbers do matter, but how they help us nurture and serve people is their principal value."

Summary

People are the strength and the greatest potential for weaknesses in an organization. An attitude of leaders and managers that embraces people as a fun and exciting part of their world is essential. People can rarely rise above those who are unwilling to embrace them in learning with and teaching them. A right attitude makes the complete difference.

Great leaders are
almost always
great simplifiers
who can cut through
argument, debate, and doubt
to offer a solution
everybody can understand.

—General Colin Powell

13. THE GATHERING MOMENT

Ready to start the journey

"You're starting the journey to operational excellence. No organization ever gets there, but they see glimpses of it along the way. The silhouette is in the distance to entice and motivate. The beauty created along the way keeps assuring everyone that the journey is worth it. Enjoy every moment.

"The meeting to announce this should be an off-site lunch meeting with a presentation. I have a set of slides for you to use, or I'll present them with you. It must be an interactive session with lots of time for Q&A, with as many questions and comments as they wish. I have some reading material for you to help you better express why you want to do this and also a schedule of how it will be done.

"It helps to open the session with team members taking the brief assessment. This will help them get to a basic understanding of the need. They can take the more complete assessment on the website after this introduction. We'll also give them some reading material to take home and an agenda and milestones that covers the first six months. It must be received as a slow and casual schedule, with the flexibility to speed it up as needed."

Diane says, "Taking on a new initiative of any type puts stress on people. Letting them know as much about how it will be done is as important as what will be done. Let them know it's about putting in place a leadership and management system and we'll work on it an hour a week. Each month, we'll have an hour-long meeting and summarize where we are, and where we're going next. I know I have a bit to learn, but I'm good at implementing change."

"I agree with you and believe you must be," responds Cal. "Change is hard because leaders want to do everything right now. Not always possible. People have old training and old habits to adjust and discard. It's not easy. In some cases, they'll have to give up what they feel made their success possible to this point."

Diane says, "I relate with that. So, if I understand this correctly, we want them to leave with a talking ability with the following key topics and themes: simplify, organize the garage, leadership and management system, online tools, and top-level thinking."

"That is right on target," says Cal. "The slide show and all the information is available at the website and can be downloaded by you for use with the team. Then we'll give them access, so they can view the demo and other training and support material that they can use as needed. If they wish, they can read a bit more, and then take a few tests and get certified at various levels to meet their needs. It's an expansive set of options, but we'll keep it as simple as possible for now."

"How much of this can we do on our own, and how much hand-holding will you have to do?" asks Diane.

"You can do the bulk of it on your own. You will need help that is available and provided on a flexible schedule. I do most of my coaching on this type of work remotely, so I don't have to be on your company premises often to make this work. The online tools provide gateways for me to be a part of all you're doing and know where you are with implementing the concepts and tools. At the start, it will take a few hours a week, and will then taper off after that. I would like to share this quote from Bill Gates of Microsoft with you.

"Everyone needs a coach. It doesn't matter whether you're a basketball player, a tennis player, a gymnast, or a bridge player."

Cal continues, "I do wish he had also included rich CEO in the list. I say this to make the point that being focused on how much you do it on your own could reduce the speed with which your team grasps it. Also, consider that it may impact how well they apply it.

"In a recent Executive Coaching Survey out of Stanford University and The Miles Group, CEOs suggest that there is interest in receiving coaching to help develop leadership sharing/delegation as well team-building skills. Use of the Zynity Leadership™ Methodology and online tools helps develop both of these. It is important to note that the survey was for larger companies and not just smaller companies.

"The cost of great advice is small compared to the cost of mistakes made without it. The cost shows up in a different set of accounting expense categories, so it hides well."

"No, I get that. And I do understand we'll need help with it. I want to make sure we're both sensitive to the need to make this happen and, at the same time, aware of how the others are doing as well."

Cal says, "Agreed. We'll work within individual schedules when working with each one on your team."

Summary

Initiating anything new begins with engaging people with the why, what, and how it will be implemented. Relax, and go slowly. It can't be done in a day. No pressure; just do it, and relax while doing it. Don't focus on mistakes. Correct them with, "No, let's do it this way for a while, and then change if we need to."

A REMINDER

A shared comprehensive perspective

The process of implementing the Zynity Leadership™ framework in an organization to establish a comprehensive top-level leading and managing system that permeates an entire organization will transform the people and the organization. Getting the various teams connected and using the online tools to share their information removes walls and builds bridges. It establishes a system for both the top level and the midlevel of the organization.

It also establishes an open culture that allows everyone to work together and pull in the same direction. Implementing the big parts and weaving them throughout the entire operating fabric of your organization will transform it and everyone in it. It establishes a consistency of ongoing improvement that nurtures innovation.

The online tools provide a system of tools to collect the proper information, and then assist users in displaying the right information at the right time. It helps make the information accessible and usable in a collaborative leadership and management environment. The big parts of the top level and their interaction with the midlevel of an organization involve a number of non-routine types of tasks, decisions, and behaviors.

Online Tools

Most Internet-based systems, to this point, are either midlevel or operating-level focused, such as CRM and accounting, where the tasks are routine and repeatable. The online tools for Zynity Leadership™ are focused on structuring top-level tasks, decisions, and behaviors that are not always routine and repeatable. This flexibility still provides consistency for top-level leadership to connect with and enhance the midlevel leadership and management requirements as well.

The big parts and the information for them are about principles and strategies. The online tools record how all connected parties use the information. This accelerates learning about what is going on in the other functional parts easier, without having to bury one another in detail. This is a key design feature of Zynity Leadership™ and the online tools.

The Human Touch

The human side of this is determining which data gets entered into the system. The machine side of this is collecting and displaying the information needed for collaborating and decision making on request. This allows us to support the non-routine tasks and decisions of the top level and the midlevel.

People will share a common perspective of the organization with their leader. They will build a workable understanding of how it all fits together and how it should work together. They will see it as the leader sees it. This alone will add significantly to the quality of daily operations, adaptation, and preparations for the future.

No one gets ignored. The process of implementing the methodology requires that everyone participate. It takes all parties to keep advancing the learning and evolving so they can accomplish more, have more fun, and…

work together in harmony!

ACKNOWLEDGMENTS

Albie and Helen Pearson have invested many hours in encouraging and mentoring me in significant ways. Their contributions and friendship have shaped and influenced me and my family in all dimensions of our lives.

As a young man in my small and much loved hometown, playing baseball was a very important part of my life. In high school my role model as a baseball player was Albie Pearson. This started when he was named Rookie of the Year in the American League while playing centerfield for the Washington Senators professional baseball team. We shared a very important feature; we are both height challenged. In 1990 I had the great blessing of meeting Albie and his wife Helen. We quickly became golf buddies. Since his successful baseball career, Albie and Helen have counseled and served many people in their roles as Christian pastors, evangelists, and servants. I am much honored to be one of those who receive their special attention.

I also give a sincere thank-you to an army of wonderful entrepreneurs and executives who have allowed me to be a confidant in their successful lives and ventures. It is always exciting to me. These exceptional people have in common a great passion to become better every day and have included teaching me along the way. They have been willing to adopt a deliberate and methodical system to guide and implement their extraordinary organizations.

134 | A FRAMEWORK FOR LEADING

ENCOURAGERS

Without whom this would not be

I appreciate much the following people who have provided specific and wonderful suggestions to make this book better: Tom Anton, PGA professional; James S. Berry, PhD; Stephen Callahan; Douglas Marshall; James A. Miller; Mark Miller; Mike Mitchell; Will Neitzke; Ralph Palmen; Andrew Pinch; Ron Sciarro; and Wayne B. Smith.

My encouragers, friends, and associates who have helped in improving the methodology, tools, and the full book series are: David B. Abright; Susan Anderson; Tom Anton, PGA professional; David Auterson; Pamela Barker; Nelson Baxley; James S. Berry, PhD; Chris Black; Anne Marie Blankenship; John Bower; Tom Bradburn; Robert H. Breinholt, PhD; Keith Burns; Stephen Callahan; Janet Canova; Joel Cash; Chris Cole; Cary C. Covert; Robby Culbreath; Dennis Eastham; Adriana Enloe; Mike Ennis; Scot Foss; David

Fried; Allen Gjersvig; Jeremy Goodman, Esq.; Hayford Gyampoh; Patrick Harter; Richard A. Herzog; Malcolm Hilcove; Al Hubbard; Lawrence A. Husick, Esq.; Dewey James; Donna James; James James; Vanessa Joaquim; Jon Kaplan; Steve Katz; Tara Kellerhals; Glen Kerby; H. William Knapp; Gene Konstant; Michael T. Kutzman, Esq.; Jennifer Levine; Allen Lorenzi; Douglas Marshall; Rick Marshall; Patrick McCalla; Don McCormick; Bill F. Miller; James A. Miller; Mark Miller; Mike Mitchell; Joseph Morehouse; Scott Morehouse; Terry Mullane; Will Neitzke; Jim Nissen Sr.; Jim O'Connor; Timothy Olp; Ralph Palmen; Larry Parsons; Paul Palmer; Deborah Peck, PhD; Cary Peters; Scott A. Peters; Kent Petzold; Andrew Pinch; Nick Puente; JoAn Risdon; Ron Sciarro; Gary G. Small; Wayne B. Smith; Dan Spencer; Brent Spore; Mike Stowell; Daniel Stringer; Jeff Struble; Eric Taylor; Jami Throne; Richard E. Upshaw (F&B); Lisa Villaluna; Laura Whitson; Don Wiest; Brandon Willey; Craig Williamson; Michael Wilmet; and Kent Wilson. Quite a village!

My children, Laura, Ryan, and Stephen, have given much and are great encouragers. I'm especially thankful to my wife, Janet, for the support, input, and commitment to our personal lives and professional careers. She is the most influential and patient teacher in my life. She is my most ardent supporter and sincerest critic in the very best sense. Much of the foundational thinking for this book has come from questions and insights she shared as we partnered together in our many entrepreneurial ventures.

Thank you all for your caring, understanding, and encouragement. I'm hopeful this book and its related materials bring happiness and value to you and to many others.

THE AUTHOR

Dwaine Canova is an international entrepreneur who started and grew his own companies and is now helping others grow theirs. Clients of his companies included IBM, Sun Microsystems, Pacific Bell, Qwest, Bell South, JC Penney, Sears, NTT (Japan's largest telephone company), Godiva, and hundreds of other international and regional companies.

In this practical book, he unveils a methodology that can be used by organizations of every type and size to improve how individuals work together. He is the founder of three companies; all became notable in their fields. He has served as CEO of two other companies and COO of two more. He built one company from napkin notes to over three thousand employees, operating in five countries with dozens of billion-dollar, multinational companies as clients and alliance partners. He has helped in the development and growth of many other organizations.

Mr. Canova is the CEO of Zynity, LLC, the developer and provider of the online SaaS (Software-as-a-Service) tools to help management teams perform their day-to-day activities more effectively. He is also the CEO of Framework for Leading Institute, LLC, a nonprofit organization that conducts and funds research in leadership.

He has spoken around the world on leadership development and the "why" and "how" of leveraging information to improve customer acquisition, retention, and service. Mr. Canova's speech to the Stanford Alumni Association is sold as part of the association's video series entitled *Executive Briefings*. The title of the video is *Customer-Focused Companies: Using Integrated Marketing Practices to Increase Profitability*.

Mr. Canova is the author of four other books in the *A Framework for Leading*™ series as well as *Overcoming the Four Deceptions in Career Relationships*, a motivational book that encapsulates his experience with and observations on interpersonal communication in organizations. It provides understanding and techniques designed to help people work more effectively together.

He has an MBA from The Wharton School, University of Pennsylvania, where he was also a teaching fellow, as well as a BS in agronomy from California State University, Fresno.

THE ASSESSMENT

Are the leadership and management capabilities as strong as you want and need them to be in your organization?

Are you open to learning more about this?

The brief assessment, which can be accessed at www.Zynity.com, will let you know how well *you* think you're doing on each item. The information in this series of books, along with the use of the related online tools, will give you the needed guidance to make significant improvements

More information about the assessment can be obtained at the www.Zynity.com website. Once at the Home Page, click on The Assessment link, and it will take you through a process and demo of the assessment tool.

This brief version allows you to have more insight about your organization and how well it currently implements these four top-level big parts:

- Strategies

- Customers

- Managing Team

- Measurements

CONTACT DWAINE

dwaine@DwaineCanova.com

To get the latest Zynity Leadership™ updates, visit:

www.ZynityLeadership.com

Dwaine speaks frequently on a variety topics including: top-level leadership and management, Zynity Leadership™, early-stage and emerging-growth companies, leadership, managership, mentoring, coaching, and entrepreneurship. He provides full-day, half-day, or keynote versions on these topics. If you want to find out more, please visit his speaking page at:

DwaineCanova.com/speaking

You can also connect with Dwaine at:

Blog: DwaineCanova.com

Twitter: twitter.com/dwainecanova

Facebook: facebook.com/dwainecanova

Blog: ZynityLeader.com

Twitter: twitter.com/ZynityLeader

Dwaine's Mission: Serving leaders and managers[1]

[1]Serving is helping, responding, anticipating,
and encouraging with full attention
to another's best interests.

Using the *Framework for Leading*™ methodology

Teaching materials are available to companies that would like to implement this on their own or with the help of *Zynity Leadership*™ Certified Partners. Please connect with us at the following website:

www.ZynityLeadership.com

Ask for information via chat or e-mail, or call the telephone number provided.

CERTIFIED PARTNERS

Certified Partners are individuals who help organizations implement and use the *Framework for Leading*™ methodology and online tools. They are listed on the company's website so that organizations can reach out to them when they need help in implementing the methodology.

Individuals who would like to become certified as partners are invited to visit the website and follow the path indicated to apply for certification. On the website, you'll receive directions regarding how to obtain thorough training on the methodology, concept, and practical implementation of the *Zynity Leadership*™ online tools. You'll have access to the necessary set of materials and be included in the referral network for coaching/consulting opportunities in your area.

There are a limited number of certifications planned for each area. There is no exclusivity available for specific geographic areas.

If you would like to apply to become a certified partner, please go to the website and follow the instructions, or e-mail us at:

partners@ZynityLeadership.com

A FRAMEWORK FOR LEADING™ SERIES

Other books being prepared for this series…

Available fall of 2015
A Framework for Leading: Customers

(Designing Organizations to Serve Customers)

This book will present how the Zynity Leadership™ methodology enhances the organization's ability to attract, engage, and serve its customers. The concepts, principles, and tools guide the development and processes necessary for the organization to structure itself explicitly around how it serves its customers.

Available winter of 2015
A Framework for Leading: Measurements

(Measuring and Managing the Right Things)

This book will present how the Zynity Leadership™ methodology enhances identifying, measuring, and managing the right things within an organization. The concepts, principles, and tools help focus individuals in organizations on the right issues at the right times. This makes it easier to work together better and perform at their highest levels.

For more information, address requests to:

books@DwaineCanova.com

books@ZynityLeader.com

Made in the USA
Columbia, SC
21 September 2021